Better Spelling in

5 Minutes a Day

Fun Spelling Activities for Kids and Parents on the Go

Mark Pennington

PRIMA PUBLISHING
3000 Lava Ridge Court • Roseville, California 95661
(800) 632-8676 • www.primalifestyles.com

The 5 MINUTES A DAY logo is a trademark of Prima Communications, Inc. PRIMA PUBLISHING and colophon are trademarks of Prima Communications Inc., registered with the United States Patent and Trademark Office.

Interior illustrations by Susan Sugnet

Library of Congress Cataloging-in-Publication Data
Pennington, Mark (Mark Frank)
    Better spelling in 5 minutes a day : fun spelling activities for kids and parents on the go / Mark Pennington
        p. cm. -- (5 minutes a day series)
    Includes index.
    ISBN 0-7615-2430-4
    1. English language--Orthography and spelling--Juvenile literature. I. Title: Better spelling in five minutes a day. II. Title. III. Series.
PE1143.P39 2001
428.1--dc21   00-065266

01 02 03 04 II 10 9 8 7 6 5 4 3 2 1
Printed in the United States of America

How to Order

Single copies may be ordered from Prima Publishing, 3000 Lava Ridge Court, Roseville, CA 95661; telephone (800) 632-8676, ext. 4444. Quantity discounts are also available. On your letterhead, include information concerning the intended use of the books and the number of books you wish to purchase.

Visit us online at www.primalifestyles.com

This book is dedicated to my own three spelling bee champions—Matt, Ryan, and Kenny—and my ever-supportive wife, Suzanne.

Contents

Acknowledgments

Special thanks to Karen Hayashi, Elementary Reading Coordinator for Elk Grove Unified School District, for her expertise and professionalism. Additional thanks to all of the terrific teachers at Markofer Elementary School, who are always willing to try something new to improve their craft. Their feedback and experimentation with my spelling ideas in their own classes has made this book a better resource for parents, teachers, and students.

I would also like to acknowledge Louisa Moats and Shane Templeton for their contributions to spelling research and effective practice. Their work has molded my understanding of sound-spelling relationships and developmental spelling.

Introduction

The local burger joint in my town has a large street sign advertising its specials. Every week, a new special is posted—and every week, the street sign has a new spelling mistake on it. The owner is not illiterate. He knows that poor spelling draws attention and that his sign sells burgers.

Why is poor spelling so noticeable? Like it or not, spelling is perceived as the indicator of academic success. Yes, Albert Einstein was a terrible speller. But Einstein and others like him have not changed the way society judges poor spellers. Poor spelling is, in fact, the most often recognized sign of illiteracy.

So why are so many smart people such poor spellers? We don't know for sure, but we do know that students learn to spell in a developmental process. This means that students learn to spell in a predictable pattern. Students first acquire oral language and the basic grammar of English. Then, students start connecting the sound-symbol relationships of our alphabetic system and begin to read and spell. If this developmental process is not appropriately nurtured, then even the most intelligent student can experience spelling difficulties.

Throughout the late 1980s and 1990s many students did not receive appropriate developmental spelling instruction. During this "whole language" movement, spelling was relegated to the role of proofreading. Many teachers provided little, if any, direct instruction in the traditional spelling patterns and rules. As a result, our society has harvested a generation of poor spellers. Standardized test spelling scores are down to historic lows. Employers and secondary teachers have complained that "Johnny can't spell."

Even today, as spelling workbooks and conventional spelling are creeping back into style in America's classrooms, teachers often admit that their weekly spelling instruction consists of Test, Study, Test, and then Forget. Very few teachers individualize their spelling program to meet the needs of each student. To be fair, most teachers have had very little training in how to teach spelling, and large class sizes can make individualization difficult. As the cycle of language arts education swings back to a more balanced approach, books like *Better Spelling in 5 Minutes a Day* can be an especially useful resource for concerned parents to help improve the spelling of their intermediate-age children.

Unlike other spelling workbooks, this book actually teaches you, the parent, how best to help your child learn spelling, without all of the teacher jargon. It follows a flexible, user-friendly approach that allows you to pick any activity whenever you have an extra 5 minutes with your child. Throughout this book, memory techniques help your child remember why a word is spelled the way it is, and Teaching Tips walk you through the best ways to ensure that your child learns each rule. At the Kitchen Table and On the Go activities give your child the practice needed for mastery of each spelling rule, using an interactive approach that is fun, quick, and easy to understand. On Your Own sections provide additional activities for your child to extend his or her learning.

Better Spelling in 5 Minutes a Day works on its own or alongside any school spelling program to help your child become an expert speller. The book starts with a simple pretest in chapter 1 to help you determine which spelling rules your child needs to develop. Chapter 1 also introduces Rules That Rock: The Sweet Sixteen. These are the spelling patterns and rules that intermediate-age children most need to master for spelling success. In chapters 2 through 4, each spelling pattern and rule is thoroughly explained in a highly memorable form with plenty of interactive and independent practice activities.

Chapter 5 presents the Super Spelling Study Plan, which will help your child learn the most effective strategies both for studying spelling words and placing these words into his or her long-term memory. Chapter 6 includes activities to help your child incorporate correct spelling in everyday writing. Your child will learn how to use The Sound-Spellings Chart and other proofreading techniques to spell even the most difficult words. The appendixes provide spelling word lists to supplement your child's weekly spelling list. The lists include frequently used words, elementary spelling toughies, commonly confused words, outlaw words, and common prefixes and suffixes, with explanations and tips for parents.

Better Spelling in 5 Minutes a Day gives you the tools to help your intermediate-age child spell with confidence. You will learn which spelling words your child most needs to know to achieve spelling success. Your child's teacher and, more importantly, your child will notice the difference that just a few minutes a day can make.

Chapter 1

Learning by the Rules

In This Chapter

- Magic 30 Spelling Test: Strengths and Weaknesses
- Rules That Rock: The Sweet Sixteen

MAGIC 30 SPELLING TEST: STRENGTHS AND WEAKNESSES

Parents' Corner

Most spelling instruction in today's classrooms is done "whole class." This means that everyone, no matter what his or her spelling ability, is taught in the same way. Children are not taught according to their individual spelling needs. But a child who is below grade level in spelling ability needs more practice in the specific areas not yet mastered—in other words, needs to catch up while still learning along with the rest of the students. A child who is above grade level in spelling ability needs targeted practice in specific spelling patterns to improve; simply adding on extra "challenge words" will not help his or her spelling. The most efficient way to teach spelling patterns is by using the rules shown to be most effective.

This chapter will help you find out what your child already knows about these spelling rules. The Magic 30 Spelling Test is designed to indicate which spelling rules your intermediate-age child has and has not yet mastered. Each of the spelling patterns most important for your intermediate-age child to master has two test items. By design, some of the words on the test will not be familiar to your child. After your child takes this quick test, you will understand very well what he or she does and does not know about these rules. Then you can develop a "game plan" to teach the spelling rules that will make a real difference in your child's spelling ability.

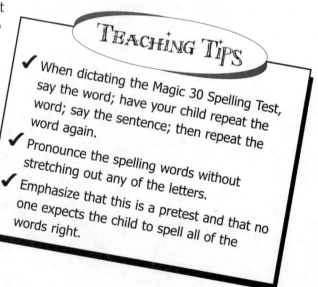

TEACHING TIPS

✔ When dictating the Magic 30 Spelling Test, say the word; have your child repeat the word; say the sentence; then repeat the word again.

✔ Pronounce the spelling words without stretching out any of the letters.

✔ Emphasize that this is a pretest and that no one expects the child to spell all of the words right.

MAGIC 30 SPELLING TEST

Get a piece of lined paper and number it from 1 to 30. Then, have a parent dictate this spelling test to you.

Rule #1

1. conceive   I can't *conceive* of a better meal.   conceive

2. believe   I *believe* what my friend told me.   believe

Rule #2

3. ledge   The book almost fell off the *ledge.*   ledge

4. courage   It takes *courage* to tell the truth.   courage

Rule #3

5. kitchen   Our family eats in the *kitchen*.   kitchen

6. conviction The *conviction* put him in jail for one year.   conviction

Rule #4

7. poison   The *poison* was stored in the garage.   poison

8. enjoyed   I *enjoyed* seeing my cousin again.   enjoyed

Rule #5

9. scratch   She had to *scratch* her name off the list.   scratch

10. touching   The dog's tail was *touching* the wet paint.   touching

Rule #6

11. passing   The driver was *passing* the truck.   passing

12. buffed   Mom *buffed* the silver plate to a shine.   buffed

Rule #7

13. classic   The song was a *classic* from the 1950s.   classic

14. checkers   My favorite game is *checkers.*   checkers

Rule #8

15. heroes   Real *heroes* are those who do their best.   heroes

16. loaves   The fresh *loaves* of bread smelled delicious.   loaves

Rule #9

17. already	I *already* finished my homework.	already
18. until	I won't see you *until* tomorrow.	until

Rule #10

19. lonesome	It gets *lonesome* out on the island.	lonesome
20. changeable	The weather is very *changeable*.	changeable

Rule #11

21. happiness	All she looked for was *happiness*.	happiness
22. monkeys	The *monkeys* are my favorite animals.	monkeys

Rule #12

23. forgetting	Aren't you *forgetting* something?	forgetting
24. exciting	Flying an airplane must be *exciting*.	exciting

Rule #13

25. tolerance	To have *tolerance* is to have respect.	tolerance
26. interference	The radio *interference* made it hard to hear.	interference

Rule #14

27. perfectible   Not everything in life is *perfectible.*   perfectible

28. breakable   The statue is *breakable.*   breakable

Rule #15

29. explosion   An *explosion* destroyed the building.   explosion

30. magician   A *magician* knows all about magic.   magician

IMAGINE THAT!

The 100 most frequently used words today come from Old English. The spellings and pronunciations have changed a lot in 800 years. That's why so many of our common words seem to be spelled so strangely.

TEST CORRECTION AND MASTERY

When you've finished, have your parent help you correct the test. Work carefully to mark any errors. This will help you find out where you can improve! As you correct the test, you and your parent can note which spelling rules you have not yet mastered. Don't worry about mistakes! You're just beginning your adventure. For words that you spelled correctly, you can skip the rule or do a few activities in the following lessons as a quick review.

RULES THAT ROCK: THE SWEET SIXTEEN

Parents' Corner

Rules That Rock: The Sweet Sixteen will be a resource that you and your child will return to over and over again. These rules have been carefully selected for the developmental spelling stages of your intermediate-age child. They have been chosen because they *work* almost all the time and because they have relatively few exceptions. Most important, they are the rules that will best inform your child's spelling decisions as a writer. These spelling rules will be a useful reference tool for some of the most difficult spelling words.

In chapters 2 through 4, each rule is introduced in a multisensory approach with plenty of clear examples, tips for teaching, and activities to help reinforce the rule for your child. Each rule is presented as concisely as possible in a memorable manner. Practice with these rules will help refine your child's spelling decisions and increase your child's confidence in writing.

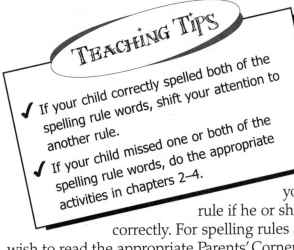

TEACHING TIPS

✓ If your child correctly spelled both of the spelling rule words, shift your attention to another rule.
✓ If your child missed one or both of the spelling rule words, do the appropriate activities in chapters 2–4.

For each spelling rule that your child has not yet mastered, do the appropriate activities in chapters 2–4. You'll know if your child has mastered the rule if he or she spells both pretest words correctly. For spelling rules already mastered, you may wish to read the appropriate Parents' Corner for that rule, read the rule with your child, and then briefly review some of the activities with your child.

AT THE KITCHEN TABLE

THE SWEET SIXTEEN

Browse through the following rules with your parent. Make a copy of The Sweet Sixteen to put in your notebook binder for spelling reference. In chapters 2, 3, and 4, you'll review these rules in detail.

1. **"i" Before "e":** In most cases, "i" comes before "e" *(believe)*, except after "c" *(receive)* or when sounded as $\bar{a}$ *(neighbor, weigh)*.

2. **The "ge" or "dge" Ending:** The final *j* sound in a word or syllable is usually spelled "dge" when it follows a short vowel *(edge)*. It is spelled "ge" when it follows a long vowel *(age)* or other vowel sounds *(large)*.

3. **The Starting *k* Sound:** The starting *k* sound is usually spelled "k" when followed by "i" or "e" *(Kim* or *Ken)* but "c" when followed by "o," "u," or "a" *(cool custom car)*.

4. **"oy" vs. "oi":** The *oi* sound is usually spelled "oy" if it's at the end of a syllable *(joyful);* otherwise, it's spelled "oi" *(rejoice)*.

5. **"ch" or "tch":** The final *ch* sound is usually spelled "tch" after short vowels in one-syllable words *(itch)*. Spell "ch" after consonants *(bunch),* long vowels *(coach),* or other vowel sounds *(couch)*.

6. **Double "l," "f," "s," and "z":** The letters "l," "f," "s," and "z" are usually doubled when they follow a short vowel at the end of a syllable *(hill, buff, pass, buzz)*.

7. **The Final *k* Sound:** The final *k* sound is usually spelled "ck" in accented short-vowel syllables *(sickly)* but "c" in unaccented short-vowel syllables *(basic)*. The *k* sound is usually spelled "k" when it follows long vowels *(bike)* or other vowel sounds *(book)*.

8. **Plurals:** For plurals, add "s" to most nouns *(cat/cats)*, including most nouns ending in "y" *(boy/boys)* or in a vowel and then an "o" *(radio/radios)*. Add "es" to the sounds of *ch, sh, s, x,* and *z* *(fox/foxes)* and to nouns ending in a consonant and then an "o" *(hero/heroes)*. For most words, change the "y" to "i" and add "es" when the noun ends in a consonant and then a "y" *(lady/ladies)*. For most nouns, change the "fe" or "lf" ending to "ves" *(wife/wives, self/selves)*.

9. **Drop the "l":** Drop one "l" from the syllables *all, till,* and *full* when adding them to other word parts *(already, until, careful)*.

10. **The Silent "e":** When attaching an ending to a word that ends with a silent "e," drop the "e" if the ending begins with a vowel *(edge/edging)*. If the ending begins with a consonant, keep the "e" *(wise/wisely)*. Also keep the "e" if the ending is "ous" or "able" following a soft *c* or *g* sound *(noticeable, courageous)* or if the end of the root word is "ee," "oe," or "ye" *(seeing, canoeing, eyeing)*.

11. **The Final "y":** If a word ends in a vowel and then a "y," keep the "y" and add the ending *(play/played)*. If a word ends in a consonant and then a "y," change the "y" to "i" and add the ending *(beauty/beautiful)*, but keep the "y" if the ending begins with an "i" *(baby/babyish)*.

12. **Consonant Doubling:** To decide whether to double a consonant when adding an ending, ask yourself three questions:
    - Does the word end with a vowel followed by a consonant? *(forget)*
    - Does the ending begin with a vowel? *(ing)*
    - Is the accent on the last syllable? *(for/get')*

If the answer to all three questions is yes, double the consonant *(forgetting)*.

Common exceptions: The "fit" and "fer" root words *(benefit/benefiting, differ/differed)* don't usually double their consonants when adding on endings.

13. **"ance" or "ence":** End a word with "ance," "ant," or "ancy" if the root contains a hard *c* or *g* sound *(significance, elegance)*, if the root can end with "ation" *(irritation/irritant)*, or if the root ends with "ear" or "ure" *(appearance, assurance)*. End a word with "ence," "ent," or "ency" if the word contains a soft *c* or *g* sound *(innocence, intelligent)*, after "id" *(confidence)*, or if the root ends with "ere" *(interference)*.

14. **"able" or "ible":** Use "able" after a hard *c* or *g* sound *(applicable, navigable)*, to follow a complete root word *(readable)*, to follow a silent "e" *(changeable)*, or if the root can end with "ation" *(irritation/irritable)*. End a word with "ible" after a soft *c* or *g* sound *(invincible, eligible)*, after an "ss" *(permissible)*, or after an incomplete root word *(visible)*.

15. **"sion," "cian," or "tion":** The final *zyun* sound is usually spelled "sion" *(explosion)*. The final *shun* sound is usually spelled "sion" when after an "l" or "s" *(compulsion, passion)*, "cian" when the word represents a person *(magician)*, and "tion" *(motion)* in most other cases.

16. **When in Doubt, Guess!**

Chapter 2

Rules That Rock

In This Chapter

- Making Friends with "i" and "e"

- Sounds Like *j*—But Not Spelled That Way

- Keeping Cool with the *k* Sound

- Ships Ahoy! Come Join the Fun!

MAKING FRIENDS WITH "I" AND "E"

Parents' Corner

Rule #1: "i" Before "e"—In most cases, the "i" comes before "e" (*believe*), except after "c" (*receive*) or when sounded as $\bar{a}$ (*neighbor*, *weigh*).

The "ie" and "ei" spellings are difficult for people of all ages. The "i" before "e" rule memory poem is the best known of all spelling rules. Remember how it goes?

> "i" before "e," except after "c," unless sounding like $\bar{a}$ as in *neighbor* or *weigh*.

This rhyme has, no doubt, saved you more than once from a misspelling. The problem is that most rules have exceptions, or words that don't fit. Exceptions to this rule are few but include some very common words, such as *weird*.

Another problem is that the classic version of the memory poem for this rule gives examples only for "sounding like $\bar{a}$ (*neighbor*, *weigh*)." It does not include an example for "ie," nor does it actually tell how to spell the "after 'c'" exception. Try this newer version of the rhyme with your child instead:

Teaching Tips

✔ Practice The "i" Before "e" Memory Poem until your child has it memorized.

✔ Ask your child to give examples of each part of the rule.

✔ Challenge your child to think of exceptions to the rule, such as *weird*, *neither*, *either*, *height*, *forfeit*, *caffeine*, *foreign*, *seize*, *their*.

The "i" Before "e" Memory Poem
"i" before "e," like *believe*,
Except after "c," like *receive*,
Or sounding like $\bar{a}$ as in *neighbor* or *sleigh*,
Where "e" before "i" is the way.

AMAZING ANAGRAMS

Anagrams are words with the letters all mixed up. For example, *wevi* is an anagram for the word *view*. Unmix the following words, using the "i" Before "e" rule and the clues in parentheses. Print the correctly spelled words in the blanks.

1. ficeh   (head firefighter)   _____

2. lngciei   (every room has one)   _____

3. egihwt   (a scale measures this)   _____

4. feidrn   (a real pal is one)   _____

5. itder   (means you attempted   _____
            something)

Have your parent check your answers. If you misspelled any words, repeat the memory poem and try to correct your mistakes.

Challenge

Now make up your own "ie" or "ei" Amazing Anagrams. Challenge your parent to solve them. Don't forget to use words that have "ie" or "ei" combinations.

CRAZY MAZE

Step along the path, but don't get lost! Find the stepping-stone pathway from **START** to **END** by drawing a line through the stones with correctly spelled words. This is a great way to get better at recognizing the "ie" and "ei" words.

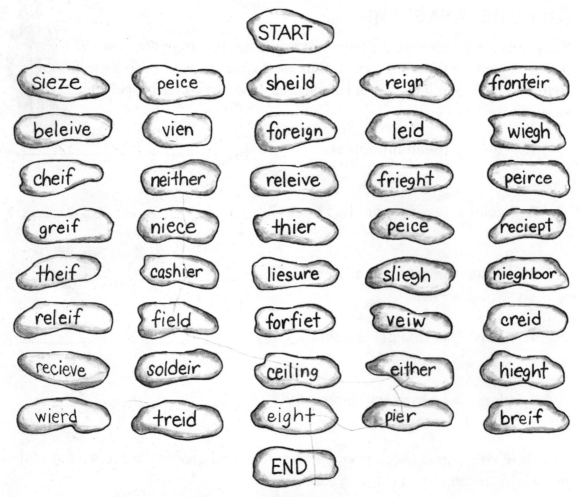

Review your solution. Make sure to refer to the memory poem if you got a bit lost.

☼ On Your Own ☼

WACKY WORD SORT

Sort the following "ie" and "ei" words into three groups using the "i" Before "e" rule. Words that don't follow the rule go in the *Weirdo Words* column. Sorting will help you see each part of the "i" Before "e" rule.

receive	neighbor	weird	relief	soldier
their	sleigh	chief	weight	field
view	either	niece	ceiling	height
friend	caffeine	eight	conceive	beige
neither	forfeit	perceive	freight	receipt

"i" Before "e"	Except After "c"	Sounding Like ā	Weirdo Words

Challenge

Now see how many words you can add to each category. Look in books or newspapers when you run out of ideas.

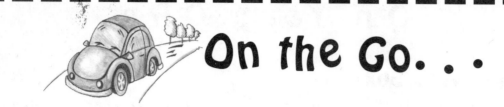

On the Go. . .

ROAD SIGN RACES

As you and your child wait for a doctor's appointment or travel through town, find words containing "ie" or "ei." For example, look in magazine advertisement, billboards, and street signs. Score 1 point for "ie" words and 2 points for "ei" words. If you find words that are exceptions to the rule, score 5 points. Go for a world record! Say the words aloud, and have your child help you keep score.

BUSY BEE SPELLING BEE

Start a one-on-one "i" Before "e" competition. Take turns with your child spelling "ie" words that follow the "i" Before "e" pattern. For example:

> **Parent:** b-e-l-i-e-v-e
> **Child:** c-h-i-e-f
> **Parent:** p-i-e-c-e
> **Child:** v-i-e-w

The first person who misspells a word or who can't think of another word gets to start the next round in which you spell words that follow the "e" before "i" pattern. After you finish with both "i" before "e" and "e" before "i," try a few exceptions.

SOUNDS LIKE J—BUT NOT SPELLED THAT WAY

Parents' Corner

Rule #2: The "ge" or "dge" Ending—The final *j* sound in a word or syllable is usually spelled "dge" when it follows a short vowel (*edge*). It is spelled "ge" when it follows a long vowel (*age*) or other vowel sounds (*large*).

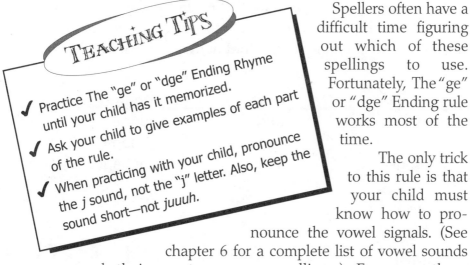

TEACHING TIPS

✓ Practice The "ge" or "dge" Ending Rhyme until your child has it memorized.

✓ Ask your child to give examples of each part of the rule.

✓ When practicing with your child, pronounce the *j* sound, not the "j" letter. Also, keep the sound short—not *juuuh*.

Spellers often have a difficult time figuring out which of these spellings to use. Fortunately, The "ge" or "dge" Ending rule works most of the time.

The only trick to this rule is that your child must know how to pronounce the vowel signals. (See chapter 6 for a complete list of vowel sounds and their most common spellings.) For now, these reminders should help:

- **Short Vowel Spellings:** *ă* in *cat*, *ĕ* in *get*, *ĭ* in *win*, *ŏ* in *box*, *ŭ* in *hug*.
- **Long Vowel Spellings:** *ā* in *cradle, rain, bay, sleigh, cake*; *ē* in *seed, bead, baby, marine, chief, complete*; *ī* in *pilot, night, try, guide, kite*; *ō* in *Ohio, oak, owner, code*; *ū* in *music, few, huge*.
- **Other Vowel Sound Spellings:** *ōō* in *boot, duty, glue, stew, dude*; *ur* in *learn, sister, bird, burn*; *ar* in *car*; *or* in *fork*; *ow* in *cow, trout*; *aw* in *hawk, author, ball*; *oy* in *soil, toy*; *ŏŏ* in *book, pudding*.

This memory rhyme might also help your child learn the rule:

The "ge" or "dge" Ending Rhyme
When words end with *j*, as in *age* or *fudge*,
There are two ways to spell them; you can be the judge:
After short vowel sounds, spell "d-g-e,"
Otherwise leave out the "d."

AT THE KITCHEN TABLE

SAY THE SECRET WORD

Using the sentence clues, select words from the following word list to fill in the blanks. After you have filled in all the words, write the letters in the boxes to discover the secret word. (Look up the secret word in the dictionary to find out what it means.)

badge	bridge	cage	dodge
edge	fudge	huge	judge
large	nudge	pages	pledge
rouge	sage	stage	teenager

1. A pet bird is kept in a ▢ _ _ _ .

2. A woman brushes on _ ▢ _ _ _ to color her cheeks.

3. Something very large would also be

called _ ▢ _ _ .

4. To move something slightly is to ▢ _ _ _ _ it.

5. An actor appears on a _ ▢ _ _ _ .

6. _ _ _ _ ▢ is a rich chocolate dessert.

> **Just for Fun!**
>
> What is at the end of everything? The letter "g."

7. A T-shirt is small, medium, or __ __ ▢ __ __ .

8. A sheriff wears a __ __ __ __ ▢ .

9. A kind of plant is ▢ __ __ __ . This is also a word for someone very wise.

10. Another word for a promise, such as when saluting the flag, is

called a ▢ __ __ __ __ __ .

11. A __ __ ▢ __ __ __ helps people cross rivers.

12. To quickly move out of the way of something is to __ ▢ __ __ __ it.

13. Someone age 13–19 is called a __ __ __ ▢ __ __ __ __ .

14. A book has many __ ▢ __ __ __ .

15. Many of the sailors with Christopher Columbus

thought that they might sail off the

__ __ ▢ __ of the earth.

16. In court, you must obey the __ __ __ __ ▢ .

Secret Word: c o u n t e r e s p i o n a g e

On Your Own

CIRCLE AND BOXING MATCH

Circle the short vowels and box the other vowel sounds in the following words. Notice how short vowels signal the ending "dge" and how long vowel and other vowel sounds signal the ending "ge."

b a d g e	a g e	f u d g e	r i d g e
h u g e	b a r g e	p l e d g e	b r i d g e
e d g e	s i e g e	r o u g e	c a g e
l a r g e	j u d g e	p a g e	s a g e

On the Go. . .

WHO'S GOT THE EDGE?

Play this game with your child while in the car or waiting somewhere in line. Take turns saying and spelling words that end in "dge." (Feel free to use proper nouns.) The last person to think of a word wins. Here are some examples:

> **Parent:** b-a-d-g-e
> **Child:** r-i-d-g-e
> **Parent:** M-i-d-g-e
> **Child:** f-u-d-g-e

Now try the same game using words that end with "ge."

RACE JUDGE

Next time you are waiting in line or out on the road, find words that end with the *j* sound. Check out billboards or the newsstand, for example. Score 1 point for each word that ends in "ge" and 2 points for each word that ends in "dge." Have your child help you keep score. Next time you go out, try to beat your previous score.

KEEPING COOL WITH THE K SOUND

Parents' Corner

Rule #3: The Starting _k_ Sound—The starting _k_ sound is usually spelled "k" when followed by "i" or "e" (_Kim_ or _Ken's_) but it is spelled "c" when followed by "o," "u," or "a" (_cool custom car_).

The _k_ sound has the unique status of being the consonant sound with the greatest number of possible spellings. For example, this sound can be written "k" (_key_), "c" (_carrot_), "qu" (_unique_), "ck" (_check_), or even "ch" (_chaos_). Because there are so many possible spellings for the _k_ sound, intermediate-age children can easily become confused about which spelling to use.

The starting _k_ sound is especially difficult. A fourth grader may have troubles spelling _ketchup_ or _catch_, while an adult may struggle with _kaleidoscope_ or _cantankerous_. Even dictionaries have changed the starting _k_ sound spellings from one letter to the other over the years to conform to popular usage.

As is most always the case with spelling rules, there are a few exceptions to The Starting _k_ Sound Rule. The starting _k_ sound spelled "ch" is limited to a few Latin derivatives, such as _chorus_ and _chemistry_; these must be memorized as sight spelling words.

TEACHING TIPS

✔ Practice the rule and the funny phrase until your child has them memorized.

✔ Ask your child to give examples, using each of the five vowels to signal the _k_ sound spellings.

✔ Explain that some words, like _chorus_ and _chemistry_, are exceptions because of their Latin derivation.

To help your child remember this rule, have him or her memorize the following funny phrase:

Kim and Ken's cool custom car.

Point out that in this phrase each word starts with the _k_ sound, but each is followed by a different one of the five vowels. The first two words are spelled with "k" and the last three with "c."

AT THE KITCHEN TABLE

THE SECRET CODE

While cracking this crazy code of English spelling, focus on the sequence of letters—especially those connecting the vowel to the *k* sound. Here's the key to the code that will help you decipher the message on the blank lines:

A = 1   C = 2   E = 3   I = 4   K = 5   O = 6   U = 7

TH3   5IT2H3N   267NT3R   4S   1   27R467S

The KITCHEN COUNTER IS A CURIOUS

PL123   T6   533P   1   L4GHT3D   21NDL3.

PLACE to Keep A LIghteD CANDLe

Challenge

Now create a secret message for your parent to decipher. Be sure to include lots of starting *k* sound words.

PYRAMID POWER

Using the clues provided to find the answers to these clues relating to the starting *k* sound. Each word is longer than the one before it. Some of the long answers are tough. You may need a parent to help you with these.

1. This vowel follows the starting *k* sound, but it isn't "e."

    A

2. Use this to unlock your door.

    key

3. A queen's husband may be this.

    King

4. It is polite to cover your mouth when you do this.

    cough

5. Take photographs with this.

    camera

6. If you want to know why something is the way it is, you are said to be this. (*Clue:* Cats are also rumored to be this.)

    Curious

7. This shows days, months, and years.

    calender

8. 1,000 meters is also called this.

    Kilometer

9. If you are sure of yourself, you are said to have this.

    Confidence

10. When you focus your attention to work hard at something, you do this.

    concentrate

11. This is the first class in elementary school.

    Kindergarten

☼n Your ☼wn

Silly Sentences

Write a sentence that includes five words starting with the *k* sound, one for each vowel ("ke," "ki," "ca," "co," and "cu"). "I like riding in Kim and Ken's cool custom car" is not as easy to create as you might think!

Imagine That!

They sound the same but have four spellings. A large diamond could be 1 *carat*. A wedding band could be 14 *karat* gold. Rabbits like *carrots*. Editors use *carets* to add in words.

Wacky Word Sort

Place each of the following word endings in either the "k" or "c" column, depending on which letter will make it a correctly spelled word. Sorting will help you practice your spelling patterns. Refer to the funny phrase "Kim and Ken's cool custom car" to make sorting choices. The first two words are already done.

Word Ending	"k"	"c"
1. itchen	kitchen	
2. atch		catch
3. eg		
4. old		
5. actus		
6. ork		
7. astle		
8. omb		
9. elp		

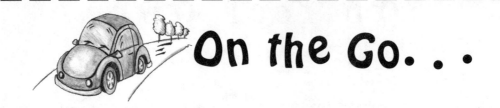

On the Go...

TEN FINGERS HAVE I

Play this game with starting *k* sound words as you and your child are driving down the road. Find five *k* sound words starting with "k," one for each finger of the left hand, on road or advertising signs. Call out the words when you see them. Then find five *k* sound words starting with "c," one for each finger of the right hand. See who can find ten words first.

THE NAME GAME

Play this game while in the car or in line somewhere. You and your child take turns saying the names of people beginning with the starting *k* sound. These names may start with "C" or with "K" but must follow the Starting *k* Sound rule. Don't just say the name; also spell it. The last person to think of a starting *k* sound name wins. Here are some examples:

> **Parent:** Cathy
> **Child:** Carrie
> **Parent:** Kenny
> **Child:** Kim

Caution! Many proper names do not follow spelling rules, so this game is going to be interesting.

SHIPS AHOY! COME JOIN THE FUN!

Parents' Corner

Rule #4: "oy" vs. "oi"—The *oi* sound is usually spelled "oy" if it's at the end of a syllable *(joyful);* otherwise, it's spelled "oi" *(rejoice).*

Students sometimes have difficulty knowing whether to spell "oy" or "oi." Fortunately, the "oy" vs. "oi" rule is one of the most consistent spelling rules. Learning when to spell "oy" and "oi" can be easy for your intermediate-age child if he or she understands how words are divided into parts, or syllables.

Syllables can provide part of the meaning of the word (like "un" in *unfinished*), or they can be simple inflections (like "ed" in *unfinished*) to change the grammatical form. Each syllable has just one vowel sound. Both the "oy" and "oi" spellings represent what we call *other vowel sounds.*

The "oy" vs. "oi" rule simply says that if the *oi* sound comes at the end of a syllable, it is spelled "oy." This is true if it comes at the end of the first syllable, as in *joyful,* or at the end of the last syllable, as in *enjoy.* If the *oi* sound comes at the start of a syllable, as in *oil,* or in the middle of a syllable, as in *joint,* it is spelled "oi."

Perhaps this memory jingle will help your child remember the "oy" vs. "oi" rule:

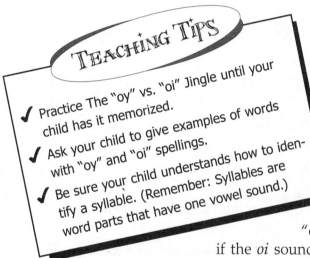

TEACHING TIPS

✓ Practice The "oy" vs. "oi" Jingle until your child has it memorized.

✓ Ask your child to give examples of words with "oy" and "oi" spellings.

✓ Be sure your child understands how to identify a syllable. (Remember: Syllables are word parts that have one vowel sound.)

> **The "oy" vs. "oi" Jingle**
> End a word part with "o-y"
> As in "j-o-y," you see.
> Everywhere else spell "o-i"
> As in "j-o-i-n-t."

AT THE KITCHEN TABLE

THE FIX-IT SHOP

This letter to Grandma really needs help. Read the letter and correct the "oy" or "oi" spelling errors right above the mistakes.

Dear Grandma,

When I turned twelve years old, I told my mom I wasn't a little boi anymore

and I was quitting school. I said, "I can get a real job doing something I

enjoi." She said, "Good luck finding a job with a boss who will emploi

someone your age."

I found a job down the street from my dad's work. Mr. Roy hired me on

the spot and put a broom in my hand. The warehouse was a rundown joynt

and smelled like rat poyson.

After a long day, I told my boss I had made a bad choyce. I had joyned the

working world too early. My mom agreed. Now I'm back in school for good.

Love,

Randy

P.S. Send more chocolate chip cookies, please.

On Your Own

CARTOON FUN

Draw a comic strip using as many "oi" and "oy" words as possible. How about "Annoying Boys" as the title?

CONNECT THE LETTERS

You won't slip up on "oy" and "oi" words after this game. Circle the correctly spelled word in each of the pairs below.

1. corduroi   corduroy

2. cowboy   cowboi

3. destroy   destroi

4. avoyd   avoid

5. foil   foyl

6. spoyl   spoil

7. convoi   convoy

8. join   joyn

9. appoint   appoynt

10. buoy   buoi

11. overjoy   overjoi

12. moist   moyst

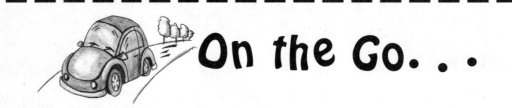

On the Go...

"A" to "Z"—And Back Again

To play this game, work through the alphabet from "A" to "Z"—to find and spell an "oi" or "oy" word starting with as many letters as possible. Take turns finding words. If you can't find one, say "pass" and give the next person a chance. If no one can find a word starting with a given letter, go on to the next letter. Score one point for every word you think of.

Examples:

A	ahoy
B	boy
C	coil
D	doily
E	enjoy

Challenge

Now try finding more words, this time starting with Z and working back to A.

Dictation Time

While you drive to an appointment or the next time you do the dishes, have your child pretend he or she is the big boss of a company. You are the assistant. As the boss, your child must dictate a letter to you. The dictated letter must contain at least six "oi" or "oy" words. During the dictation, challenge your child to spell out each "oi" and "oy" word.

Chapter 3

More Rules That Rock

In This Chapter

- Guess Which Pitch

- Double, Double, What's the Trouble?

- Back on Track with the *k* Sound

- Two of a Kind

- The Disappearing "L"

- Silence in the House, Please

- The Grand Final-"y"

GUESS WHICH PITCH

Parents' Corner

Rule #5: "ch" or "tch"—The final *ch* sound is usually spelled "tch" after short vowels in one-syllable words *(itch)*. It is spelled "ch" after consonants *(bunch)*, long vowels *(coach)*, or other vowel sounds *(couch)*.

Children who are learning to spell are often confused about when to use the "ch" or "tch" spellings for the *ch* sound. Fortunately, this rule has few exceptions. The common exceptions include *rich, which, such,* and *much.*

To apply this rule, your child must be able to recognize short vowels, long vowels, and other vowel sounds. These vowel sounds signal which spelling comes after the vowel to end the syllable. All of the basic sounds and their spellings are covered in The Sound-Spellings Chart in chapter 6. For now, the following reminders and memory verse should help:

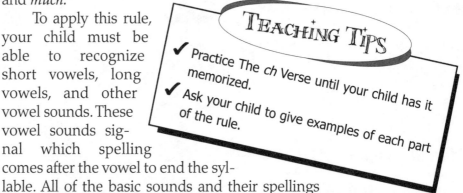

TEACHING TIPS

✓ Practice The *ch* Verse until your child has it memorized.

✓ Ask your child to give examples of each part of the rule.

- **Short Vowel Spellings (signaling "tch" spelling in a one-syllable word):** ă in *cat*, ĕ in *get*, ĭ in *win*, ŏ in *box*, ŭ in *hug.*
- **Long Vowel Spellings (signaling "ch" spelling):** ā in *cradle, rain, bay, sleigh*; ē in *seed, bead, baby, marine, chief, complete*; ī in *pilot, night, try, guide, kite*; ō in *Ohio, oak, owner, code*; ū in *music, few, huge.*
- **Other Vowel Sound Spellings (signaling "ch" spelling):** ōō in *boot, duty, glue, stew*; ur in *learn, sister, bird, burn*; ar in *car*; or in *fork*; ow in *cow, trout*; aw in *hawk, author, ball*; oy in *soil, toy*; ŏŏ in *book, pudding.*

The *ch* Verse
When ending words after short vowels,
"t-c-h" fits well.
But after every other sound,
"c-h" is just swell.

AT THE KITCHEN TABLE

BRAIN TEASERS

Fill in the blank with *ch* sound words. Each couplet rhymes. When you are done, read the rhyming pairs to your parent.

1. If you have to scratch, you have a(n) _____.

2. If you have lots of money, you must be _____.

3. If you eat ten donuts, that's way too _____.

4. If you sprain your ankle, you'll lean on a(n) _____.

5. If you guide a sports team, you're the _____.

6. Eggs you can scramble, fry, or _____.

POETS' CORNER

Write a four-line poem with a short-vowel "tch" ending for each end rhyme and any other sound "ch" ending word inside each line. Now read your poem to a parent, pausing before saying any of your *ch* sound words. How many of these words can your parent guess?

On Your Own

HIDDEN PATTERN

Shade in all of the correctly spelled "ch" and "tch" words to form the Hidden Pattern.

boch	noch	approach	pitcher	wach	coatch
attatch	match	pach	lach	touch	detatch
punch	stiches	wiches	swich	stiching	ranch
fetch	strech	skeching	cruches	pich	etching
bucher	scratched	unlach	stopwach	peach	hopscoch
poatched	roatch	clutching	hutches	sutch	mutch

IMAGINE THAT!

New words can be formed from two existing words. Everyone calls the tunnel connecting England and France across the English Channel the "chunnel"—a blend of channel and tunnel.

On the Go. . .

RAMBLING RHYMERS

Here's a game you can play anywhere and at any time. Challenge your child to the rhyming game. Start with an "atch," "etch," "itch," "otch," or "utch" word. Say the word and then spell it. Your child must say and spell a word that rhymes with your word, and then say another word. You think of a rhyming word and spell it, and so on, until someone can't think of either a rhyme or a new word. The last rhyme wins! Here's an example:

Parent: batch: b-a-t-c-h

Child: catch: c-a-t-c-h; ditch: d-i-t-c-h

Parent: itch: i-t-c-h; crutch: c-r-u-t-c-h

STREET SIGN SEARCH

While on your way to school or the store, find *ch* sounds on road or advertising signs. Each player finds words in which the *ch* sound follows either a consonant (as in *bench*), long vowel sound (*coach*) or other vowel sound (as in *couch*). The first person to find ten words that have the *ch* sound spelled with "ch" is the winner.

DOUBLE, DOUBLE, WHAT'S THE TROUBLE!

Parents' Corner

Rule #6: Double "l," "f," "s," and "z"—The letters "l," "f," "s," and "z" are usually doubled when they follow a short vowel at the end of a syllable (*hill, buff, pass, buzz*).

One of the most common spelling errors among children and adults is doubling (or not doubling) consonants. The Double "l," "f," "s," and "z" rule is useful because it works most of the time and because it is not too complicated. Common exceptions include *yes, quiz, plus, if, this, bus, gas,* and *us.* Also, if the final *f* sound is after a short vowel formed by "au" or "ou," the spelling is "gh" (*laugh, enough*). In addition, one of the "l"s is dropped in the syllables *all, till,* and *full* when adding onto another word part (see Rule #9: Drop the "l").

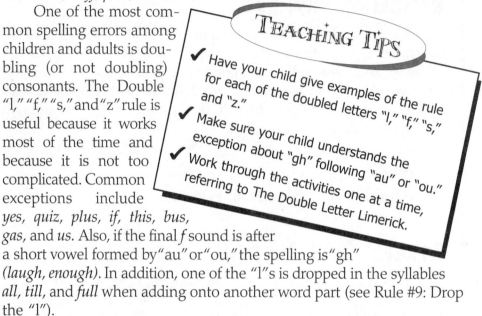

Teaching Tips

✓ Have your child give examples of the rule for each of the doubled letters "l," "f," "s," and "z."

✓ Make sure your child understands the exception about "gh" following "au" or "ou."

✓ Work through the activities one at a time, referring to The Double Letter Limerick.

To apply this rule correctly, your child must be able to recognize short vowel sounds and remember that every syllable has only one vowel sound. With this rule, a short vowel signals that the consonants "l," "f," "s," and "z" must be doubled at the end of a syllable. Review the short vowel sounds: ă in *cat,* ĕ in *get,* ĭ in *win,* ŏ in *box,* ŭ in *hug* if you think that your child needs to. The following memory limerick might also help your child remember this rule:

The Double Letter Limerick
There once was a short vowel syllable,
Who doubled "l," "f," "s," and "z,"
The rest of his vowel friends
Would usually end
With just single letters, you see.

RHYMES AND REASONS

Fill in the blanks with words from the following list, using the clues in parentheses for help.

boss	bull	bus	buzz	cough
cuff	full	fuzz	gas	grass
hiss	loss	mess	miss	off
roll	toll	tough	us	Yes

1. _____ (not *no*), you made a real _____ (unclean).

2. "_____" (sound), said the snake. "I never _____ (bad aim)."

3. The _____ (employer) was upset at our _____ (not a win)

4. Stay off the _____ (lawn), and step on the _____ (fuel).

5. His _____ (not a sneeze) knocked _____ (not on) his hat.

6. A yellow _____ (school) drove _____ (we).

7. He had a _____ (not easy) time taking off his _____ (end of a long sleeve) links.

8. The _____ (male cattle) ate a _____ (complete) field of

grass.

9. He had to give me an extra wheat dinner _____ (like bread)

because I paid for his bridge _____ (payment for crossing).

10. The bees made a loud _____ (sound) as they rubbed against

the soft _____ (like velvet) of the flowers.

POETS' CORNER

Compose a nursery rhyme using these exception words and word parts: *yes, quiz, plus, if, this, bus, gas, us,* "augh," "ough." When you have finished writing, have a poetry reading in your family. Each family member can read or recite his or her favorite poem. When it is your turn, recite your own creation!

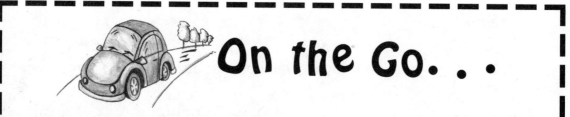

DOUBLE LETTER LOOKOUT

This game is fun to play while traveling down the road or through the grocery aisles. Look at road signs, advertising, or packages to find a word with multiple syllables in which the "l," "f," "s," or "z" letter is doubled. Set an end time—maybe when you arrive at your destination or when you have found everything on your shopping list—and see who can find the most doubles. Here are some examples:

    pulling   muffler   bosses   grizzly

On Your Own

BACKWARD (DRAWKCAB) STORY

Read the following backward story and write down the missing double "l," "f," "s," or "z" words that belong in the spaces provided.

. _ll_ ub rieht _ss_ im yllaer _ll_ iw yehT !swoc sih rof _ss_ ol hguot a

tahW . _ff_ o mih esahc ot sag eht no deppets revird eht dna emac sub

wo _ll_ ey a yad enO .dleif sih fo _ss_ ob yletinifed saw eH . _ll_ uf

saw eh litnu eta eh hcihw , _ss_ arg eht ni _ll_ or neht ,trons dna

_ss_ ih dluow eH . _ll_ ub naem yrev a saw ecno erehT

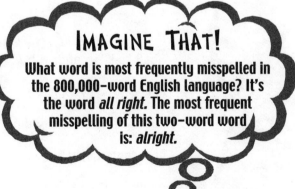

IMAGINE THAT!
What word is most frequently misspelled in the 800,000-word English language? It's the word *all right.* The most frequent misspelling of this two-word word is: *alright.*

BACK ON TRACK WITH THE K SOUND

Parents' Corner

Rule #7: Final *k* Sound—The final *k* sound is usually spelled "ck" in accented short-vowel syllables *(sickly)* but "c" in unaccented short-vowel syllables *(basic)*. The *k* sound is usually spelled "k" when it follows long vowels *(bike)* or other vowel sounds *(book)*.

The "c," "k," or "ck" rule is one of many spelling rules that depends on whether a syllable is accented or unaccented. Remember that a syllable is a word part with a vowel. An accented syllable is the part of the word that is louder, or gets more punch, than the other word part(s) (as the "POR" in imPORtant).

Help your child memorize this rule to the sound of an army drill sergeant singing a cadence to keep soldiers marching in perfect formation. To make things easy, the words of the cadence are printed in italics next to each line.

TEACHING TIPS

✓ Practice The *k* Sound Memory Drill until your child has it memorized.

✓ Ask your child to give examples of each part of the rule.

✓ Make sure your child understands the concepts of syllables and accented or unaccented syllables.

The *k* Sound Memory Drill

Spell "c-k" to end with *k**	*I don't know, but I've been told.*
in accented syllables.	*The streets of heaven are paved with gold.*
But spell "c" when ending in	*I don't know, but I've been told.*
unaccented syllables.	*The streets of heaven are paved with gold.*
Spell "k" (Spell "k")	*Sound off (Sound off)*
af-ter (af-ter)	*Here it again (Here it again)*
other vowel and	*One, Two, Three, Four*
(two beats pause)—long vowels!	*(two beats pause)—Three, Four!*

*pronounce the *k* sound, not the letter "k"

AT THE KITCHEN TABLE

LUCKY DUCK

To apply the "c," "k," or "ck" Rule, you need to recognize short, long, and other vowel sounds. Read over the following before you complete the activity.

- **Short Vowel Spellings:** ă in *cat*, ĕ in *get*, ĭ in *win*, ŏ in *box*, ŭ in *hug*
- **Long Vowel Spellings:** ā in *cradle, rain, bay, sleigh, cake;* ē in *seed, bead, baby, marine, chief, complete;* ī in *pilot, night, try, guide, kite;* ō in *Ohio, oak, owner, code;* ū in *music, few, huge*
- **Other Vowel Sound Spellings:** o͞o in *boot, duty, glue, stew, dude;* ur in *learn, sister, bird, burn;* ar in *car;* or in *fork;* ow in *cow, trout;* aw in *hawk, author, ball;* oy in *soil, toy;* o͝o in *book, pudding*

Fill in the blanks with the correct *k* sound spellings to complete this story. Then read your story to a parent.

This is the story of a little yellow du __ __ named

Lu __ __ y. She li __ ed to soa __ her long ne __ __ in the

shallow waters under the histori __ do __ __ on Millers

Pond. One day, while swimming under the do __ __ ,

Lu __ __ y heard a franti __ scream. Lu __ __ y loo __ ed up qui __ __

ly to see a boy who had just crashed his bi __ e. When the du __ __

tried to loo __ ba __ __ down, she found that her bill was stu __ __

between the do __ __ boards. In a pani __ , Lu__ __ y began to qua __ __

loudly. A nice tru __ __ driver heard the noise while driving by and

stopped to help. He too __ apart the boards to rescue Lu __ __ y. Lu

__ __ y's bill hurt for a wee __ , but she still tells this dramati __ story

to attentive young du __ __ lings on Millers Pond.

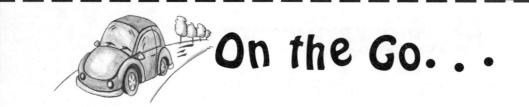

On the Go. . .

ATTENTION: K-MART SHOPPERS

The next time you are in the supermarket, have your child look at the packages to find words or syllables with other vowel sounds that end in a "k." While you are checking off items on your shopping list, your child can check off the other vowel sounds on a list that he or she makes from the list found in the At the Kitchen Table activity.

On Your Own

WACKY WORD SORT

Sort the words below into four groups according to the vowel that determines the spelling of the *k* sound: "ck" as in *sick*, "c" as in *basic*, "k" as in *cake*, or "k" as in *beak*. You'll memorize the spelling patterns more easily if you sort them out.

mosaic	make	quickly	took
stacker	terrific	looked	baking
raking	neck	black	looked
wreck	leaked	bike	back
week	dramatic	hiking	quacked
weaken	soak	book	historic
taken	frantic	raking	classic

TWO OF A KIND

Parent's Corner

Rule # 8: The Plurals Rule—For plurals, add "s" to most nouns (*cat/cats*), including most nouns ending in "y" (*boy/boys*) or in a vowel and then an "o" (*radio/radios*). Add "es" to the sounds of *ch, sh, s, x,* and *z* (*fox/foxes*) and to nouns ending in a consonant and then an "o" (*hero/heroes*). For most nouns that end in a consonant followed by a "y," change the "y" to an "i" and add "es" (*lady/ladies*). For most nouns, change the "fe" or "lf" ending to "ves" (*wife/wives, self/selves*).

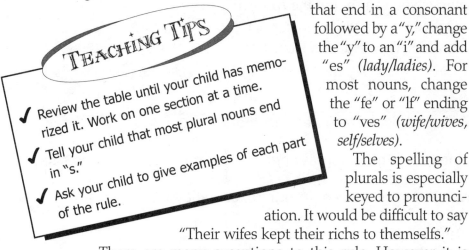

The spelling of plurals is especially keyed to pronunciation. It would be difficult to say "Their wifes kept their richs to themselfs."

There are many exceptions to this rule. However it is much easier to apply a rule that works most of the time and memorize the exceptions as sight spelling words, rather than to memorize *all* of the plural words as exceptions.

For most nouns:

If	Then
the noun ends in a vowel and then "y" the noun ends in a vowel and then "o"	add "s"
the noun ends in these sounds: *ch, sh, s, x,* or *z* the noun ends in a consonant and then "o"	add "es"
the noun ends in a consonant and and then "y"	change the "y" to "i" add "es"
the noun ends in "fe" or "lf"	change the "fe" or "lf" to "ves"

TEACHING TIPS

✔ Review the table until your child has memorized it. Work on one section at a time.

✔ Tell your child that most plural nouns end in "s."

✔ Ask your child to give examples of each part of the rule.

PLURALS ON THE FARM

See how many plurals you can find in the following story. If any are spelled wrong, write the correct word above the mistake. Then read the story to a parent.

Dan and Marie Johnson have been farmers all of their lifes. "We mostly grow peas and tomatos these days," says Dan. "They seem to grow best in our Texas valleys. We've tried potatoes, but they were just zeroes!"

"Our shelfs are full of fresh farm produce," says Marie, as she washes the last ripe tomato and places it on the shelf. She always finishes her morning dutys in the house first. Then she goes outside to help her husband. Texas wifes work as true partners with their husbands in the family farm business.

For fun, Dan and Marie like to attend the local cowboy rodeos or just stay at home to watch music videoes. Farming in Texas is hard but rewarding work.

On Your Own

WACKY WORD SORT

Sort the following words into the seven plural rule categories.

benches	berries	cities	desks	dishes
echoes	faces	lives	monkeys	patios
plays	studios	tomatoes	wolves	washes

1. nouns not covered by exceptions:

2. nouns ending in a vowel and then "y":

3. nouns ending in a vowel and then "o":

4. words ending in "ch," "sh," "s," "x," or "z":

5. nouns ending in a consonant and then "o":

6. nouns ending in a consonant and then "y":

7. nouns ending in "fe" or "lf":

CHEF'S DELIGHT

Write out a menu for breakfast, lunch, and dinner for one day. Next, make all the foods that you've listed plural. Tell your mom and dad to be prepared for French fries for breakfast and donuts for dinner. Now make out a menu for a whole week!

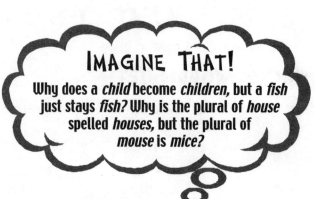

IMAGINE THAT!

Why does a *child* become *children*, but a *fish* just stays *fish?* Why is the plural of *house* spelled *houses*, but the plural of *mouse* is *mice?*

On the Go. . .

ROAD SIGN PLURALS RACE

Play this game the next time you are out driving with your child. You look for "s" endings on road or advertising signs, while your child looks for "es" endings. See who can find the most words. (*Hint:* You have a definite advantage in this one, so switch with your child after a while to keep things fair.)

TRAVELING PLURALS

While in the car, take turns with your child naming things you can see and saying them in their plural form. You might name car parts, clothes, or trash in the garbage bag—anything! Spell the plural form after you have named something, and then let the next person name something. All players will find this a greater challenge as the game progresses and they have fewer items to choose from. Here are some examples:

seatbelt/seatbelts   dashboard/dashboards

upholstery/upholsteries   radio/radios

THE DISAPPEARING "L"

Parents' Corner

Rule #9: Drop the "l" Rule—Drop one "l" from the syllables *all*, *till*, and *full* when adding them to other word parts (*already, until, careful*).

Both children and adults often forget to drop the "l" when adding the syllables *all*, *till*, and *full* to another word part. In most cases, one of the "l"s drops off when the *all*, *till*, and *full* syllable is added to the beginning of a word such as with *already* or at the ending of a word such as with *until*. Remember that both of the letter "l"s are kept following short vowels in other syllables, such as with *tell* or *still* (see Rule #6: Double "l," "f," "s," and "z").

There are a few exceptions to the Drop the "l" Rule, such as with the word *fulfill*—which drops the "l" from the first syllable, but not the last. Also, when some of the Greek and Latin affixes (prefixes and suffixes) are added on to *all*, *till*, and *fill*, both "l"s can be retained, such as with the word *refill*. In general, however, this is a very consistent and useful rule.

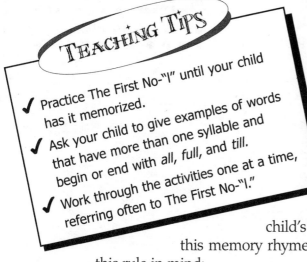

Teaching Tips

✓ Practice The First No-"l" until your child has it memorized.

✓ Ask your child to give examples of words that have more than one syllable and begin or end with *all*, *full*, and *till*.

✓ Work through the activities one at a time, referring often to The First No-"l."

Many times a simple rhyme will help place a spelling rule into your child's long-term memory. Try this memory rhyme to help your child keep this rule in mind:

The First No-"l"
With *all* and *till* and *full*
You always drop one "l"
When adding on a syllable.

AT THE KITCHEN TABLE

MATCHING MANIA

Draw lines between the word parts to complete the words.

un	most
care	ways
all	till
help	fill
all	full
full	full

Now spell each word correctly by dropping the "l" as needed.

> **Just for Fun!**
> If William's wife went to Williamstown while William washed Wally's work clothes, how many "W"s are there in all? (There are no "W"s in *all*.)

1. un _____

2. care _____

3. all _____

4. help _____

5. all _____

6. full _____

MOVIE MAGIC

Make a poster advertising your favorite movie using descriptive words that end in *all*, *till*, and *full*. Read your advertisement to a parent. Maybe your parent will want to see your *suspenseful* movie!

On Your Own

SONGWRITER'S SERENADE

Compose your own Drop the "l" song lyric to the melody of a favorite song to help you remember the rule.

AMAZING ANAGRAMS

Use the clues in parentheses to unmix the following words:

1. nopsfluo (not a forkful)   _____

2. lufceape (not warlike)   _____

3. dayelra (by this time)   _____

4. werpoluf (very strong)   _____

5. lamsto (not quite)   _____

6. syawla (every time)   _____

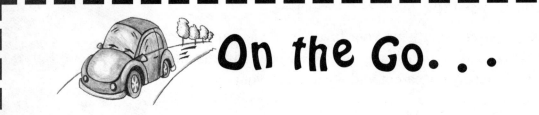

On the Go. . .

THE GREAT "L" SEARCH

While driving through town, challenge your child to see who can find the most words with more than one syllable that start or end with *all*, *till*, or *full*. It's O.K. to score twice if you find the same word twice. Whoever finds the most words before you reach your destination wins.

SILENCE IN THE HOUSE, PLEASE

Parents' Corner

Rule #10: The Silent "e" Rule—When attaching an ending to a word that ends with a silent "e," drop the "e" if the ending begins with a vowel (*edge/edging*). If the ending begins with a consonant, keep the "e" (*wise/wisely*). Also keep the "e" if the ending is "ous" or "able" following a soft *c* or *g* sound (*noticeable, courageous*) or if the end of the root word is "ee," "oe," or "ye" (*seeing, canoeing, eyeing*).

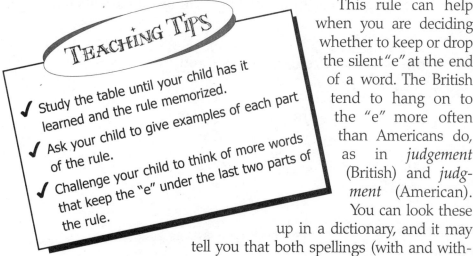

TEACHING TIPS

✓ Study the table until your child has it learned and the rule memorized.

✓ Ask your child to give examples of each part of the rule.

✓ Challenge your child to think of more words that keep the "e" under the last two parts of the rule.

This rule can help when you are deciding whether to keep or drop the silent "e" at the end of a word. The British tend to hang on to the "e" more often than Americans do, as in *judgement* (British) and *judgment* (American). You can look these up in a dictionary, and it may tell you that both spellings (with and without the "e") are acceptable. Common exceptions to the rule stated here are *truly*, *argument*, and *judgment*.

When adding on an ending to a silent *e* word:

If	Then
the ending begins with a vowel	drop the "e"
the ending begins with a consonant the ending is "ous" or "able" after a soft c or g sound the ending is "ee," "oe," or "ye"	keep the "e"

TO DROP OR NOT TO DROP

To play this game, you need a stack of blank cards (old business cards or index cards will do), a pencil, and a partner. On each of the cards, write one of the following root words or endings. Some of the endings will be on more than one card.

bake	ing	curve	ed
free	ly	tree	less
trace	able	shoe	less
glee	ful	eye	sore
care	ful	sue	ing

Now make two piles of cards, one of roots and the other of endings. Shuffle each pile separately. When it is your turn, draw one card from each pile. Tell your opponent whether you can put the two cards together to make a word and, if so, whether you need to drop the "e" from the root word. If you get a match and answer correctly about the "e," keep the pair. If not, discard and let the other player take a turn. Play until all cards have been used. If you like, you may shuffle the unused cards in their own piles and go through the stack a second time. The person with the most pairs at the end wins.

WACKY WORD SORT

Sort the following words into four columns according to whether you would drop or keep the "e" when adding an ending.

making	agreement	nicer
skating	purely	excitement
outrageous	squarely	changeable
hopeless	sized	shoestring

Drop "e" if ending begins with vowel	**Keep "e" if ending begins with consonant**	**Keep "e" with "able" or "ous" after soft *c* or *g***	**Keep "e" if root word ends with "ee," "oe," or "ye"**

Challenge

How many more words you can add to each column in the list?

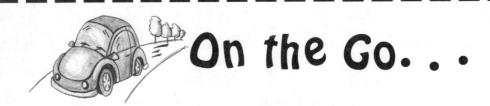

On the Go. . .

THE SILENT "E"-OR NOT?

Have your child watch for silent "e" misspellings whenever you are out and about. Unfortunately, these aren't hard to find. Look at business signs, newspaper advertisements, school newsletters, or while waiting in the *Driv Thru* fast food line.

On Your Own

SILENT SEARCH

Look at the subtitles in one of your textbooks to find words that have kept the "e" when adding on an ending. Then look for words that have *dropped* the "e" when adding on an ending. Make a list of both kinds of words. Do you find more that kept the "e" or more that dropped it?

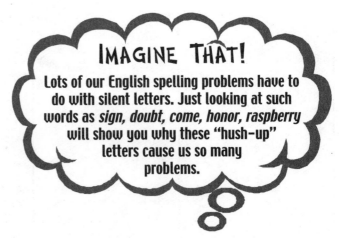

IMAGINE THAT!

Lots of our English spelling problems have to do with silent letters. Just looking at such words as *sign, doubt, come, honor, raspberry* will show you why these "hush-up" letters cause us so many problems.

THE GRAND FINAL-"y"

Parents' Corner

Rule #11: The Final "y"—If a word ends in a vowel and then a "y," keep the "y" and add the ending *(play/played)*. If a word ends in a consonant and then a "y," change the "y" to an "i" and add the ending *(beauty/beautiful)*, but keep the "y" if the ending begins with an "i" *(baby/babyish)*.

Next to "i" before "e" except after "c," change the "y" to "i" and add "es" is the spelling rule that people remember most often. Keep in mind, however, that change the "y" to "i" and add "es" is only *part* of a very useful and consistent rule. In this lesson, your child will work on learning the *whole* rule to improve his or her spelling.

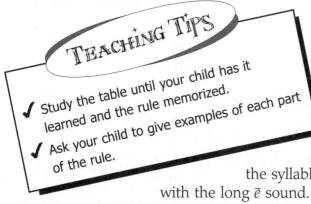

Your child needs to know that besides the common "a," "e," "i," "o," and "u" vowels, the "y" can also serve as a vowel. In the syllable "cry," the "y" is a vowel with the long ī sound; in the syllable "ly," the "y" is a vowel with the long ē sound. Knowing this will help your child identify the ending "y" syllable and be able to apply this rule.

When adding an ending to a word that ends with "y":

If	Then
The word ends in a vowel and then a "y"	Keep the "y" and add the ending
The word ends in a consonant and then a "y"	Change the "y" to "i" and add the ending
Unless The ending starts with "i"	Keep the "y"

TO CHANGE OR NOT TO CHANGE

Which of the following roots need the "y" turned into an "i" before the ending can be added? Answer Yes or No as to whether the "y" should be changed. Then spell the new word correctly.

Final "y"	Word Ending	Change "y"	New Word
1. stay	ed	_____	_____
2. carry	s	_____	_____
3. boy	s	_____	_____
4. try	ing	_____	_____
5. cherry	s	_____	_____
6. enjoy	ment	_____	_____
7. baby	ish	_____	_____
8. play	ful	_____	_____

PEN PAL

Write a letter to your parent in which you alternate final "y" words that keep the "y" when adding endings with final "y" words that drop the "y" when adding endings. You might use words like *crying*, *happiest*, and *babyish*.

On the Go. . .

STREET SIGN RACES

As you're out driving, look for words on billboards, advertisements, or truck sides in which the final "y" is kept with an ending. Have your child look for words in which the final "y" is changed to "i." After a while, switch.

On Your Own

WACKY WORD SORT

Combine the following root words with the given endings and then write each new word in the appropriate column.

Root	Ending	Consonant, then "y"	Vowel, then "y"	Consonant, then "y" but ending starts with "i"
1. say	ing	_____	_____	_____
2. toy	s	_____	_____	_____
3. journey	ed	_____	_____	_____
4. carry	ing	_____	_____	_____
5. cry	ed	_____	_____	_____
6. play	er	_____	_____	_____
7. fly	ing	_____	_____	_____
8. dry	est	_____	_____	_____

Chapter 4

And More
Rules That Roll

In This Chapter

- Compelling Spelling
- Spell with Confidence
- Able to Be Invisible
- Is It an Illusion?
- When in Doubt, Guess!

COMPELLING SPELLING

Parents' Corner

Rule #12: Consonant Doubling—To decide whether to double a consonant when adding an ending, ask yourself three questions:

1. Does the word end with a vowel followed by a consonant? *(forget)*

2. Does the ending begin with a vowel? *(ing)*

3. Is the accent on the last syllable? *(for/get')*

If the answer to all three questions is yes, double the consonant *(forgetting)*.

The consonant doubling rule will equip you and your child to spell even the most difficult words. Common exceptions: The "fit" and "fer" root words *(benefit/benefiting, differ/differed)* don't usually double their consonants when adding on endings.

Children can learn this rule to the tune of "Mary Had a Little Lamb."

TEACHING TIPS

✓ Review the three conditions of the doubling rule and the Memory Nursery Rhyme until your child has them memorized.

✓ Ask your child to give examples of the rule with words that do double the final consonant and with words that do not.

Memory Nursery Rhyme

If you have a word that ends
In a vowel-consonant,
And you add an ending that
Begins with a vowel,
And the word is accented
On the last syllable,
Double the last consonant,
if these three agree.

*Mary had a little lamb
Little lamb, little lamb
Mary had a little lamb
Whose fleece was white as snow.
And everywhere that Mary went
Mary went, Mary went,
Everywhere that Mary went, the
lamb was sure to go.*

AT THE KITCHEN TABLE

TO DOUBLE OR NOT TO DOUBLE

In the table that follows, look at the root word and the ending spelling for each line. Under "Number(s)," write the number for each condition that applies, as follows:

1. The word ends with a vowel followed by a consonant.
2. The ending begins with a vowel.
3. The accent is on the last syllable.

Finally, under "New Word," combine the root word and its ending using the correct spelling. All three conditions must be met to double the consonant. The first two are completed as samples.

Root Word	Ending	Number(s)	New Word
1. listen	ing	1, 2	listening
2. commit	ed	1, 2, 3	committed
3. fun	y	_____	_____
4. begin	ing	_____	_____
5. forget	able	_____	_____
6. stack	ing	_____	_____
7. light	ed	_____	_____
8. comic	al	_____	_____
9. permit	ed	_____	_____

DOUBLE DARE CONCENTRATION

Here's a game you can play with a parent. You'll need a stack of blank cards (index cards or old business cards) and a pencil. On each of the cards, write one of the following root words or endings:

tax	sad	drop	chair	begin
fit	pilot	prefer	drip	friend
inherit	admit	stop	confer	elder
chant	control	star	entertain	cloud
able	est	ing	s	ing
est	ing	ed	ed	ship
ance	ed	ing	ence	ly
ing	ed	y	ment	y

Shuffle all of the cards together and place them face down on a table in five rows of eight cards each. Take turns flipping two cards over at a time. If one card shows a root word and the other an ending, decide if the cards can be put together to make a word. If they can, say whether the word has a double consonant or not. If you get the answer right, keep the pair of cards for a point. If not, turn them back over—but remember where they are so you can use them later. Then it's your opponent's turn.

On Your Own

AD APPEARANCE

Look through magazine advertisements to find double consonant words for these endings:

-est   -ing   -ance   -ence   -ed   -ship   -ly   -ment   -s

Can you find at least one word that has each ending. Which ending has the most roots?

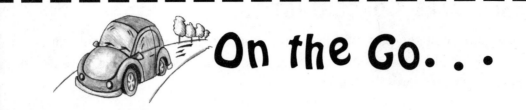

On the Go...

THE NAME GAME

While en route to your next activity, play this game with your child to practice the idea of accented syllables. Take turns giving the first names of people you know who have accents on the last syllable of their names. For example, you might have

Parent: Annette'
Child: Suzanne'
Parent: Danielle'
Child: Michelle'

Next, try thinking of names with the accent on the first syllable—or try last names.

CLAP THE SYLLABLE

While you're waiting in line, give your child words made up of roots and endings and have your child tell you whether the consonant is doubled. After he or she has answered two words correctly, let the child think of words for you to figure out. Remind your child of the three conditions listed in Parents' Corner if necessary.

Here are some words you might try:

taxable	saddest	dropping	chairs	spinning
fittest	piloting	preferred	dripped	friendship
inheritance	admitted	stopped	conference	elderly
chanting	controlled	starry	entertainment	cloudy

SPELL WITH CONFIDENCE

Parents' Corner

Rule #13: "ance" or "ence"—End a word with "ance," "ant," or "ancy" if the root contains a hard *c* or *g* sound (*significance, elegance*), if the root can end with "ation" (*irritation/irritant*), or if the root ends with "ear" or "ure" (*appearance, assurance*). End a word with "ence," "ent," or "ency" if the word contains a soft *c* or *g* sound (*innocence, intelligent*), after "id" (*confidence*), or if the root ends with "ere" (*interference*)

It has taken many years for these endings to become consistent in our spelling system. Like many of our spellings, pronunciation has helped determine how to spell each ending. That is why the soft and hard *c* or *g* sounds have such an effect on so many spelling endings.

Roots are words or word parts (like *endure*) that carry the meaning of the word when combined with prefixes and suffixes (as in *endurance*).

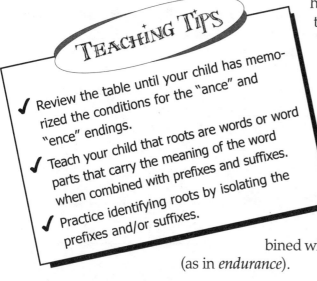

TEACHING TIPS

✓ Review the table until your child has memorized the conditions for the "ance" and "ence" endings.

✓ Teach your child that roots are words or word parts that carry the meaning of the word when combined with prefixes and suffixes.

✓ Practice identifying roots by isolating the prefixes and/or suffixes.

When deciding what ending to use:

If	Then
the root contains a hard *c* or *g* sound	
"ation" can be added to the root	end in "ance," "ant," or "ancy"
the root ends in "ear" or "ure"	
the root contains a soft *c* or *g* sound	
the root contains "id"	end in "ence," "ent," or "ency"
the root ends in "ere"	

WACKY WORD SORT

Sort these words into six categories by filling in the blanks after the numbered conditions that follow:

clearance   radiance   arrogance   negligence   reverence   coincidence

tolerant   vacant   endurance   confidence   adherence   providence

1. root contains hard *c* or *g* sound

_____   _____

2. can add "ation" to the root

_____   _____

3. root ends in "ear" or "ure"

_____   _____

4. root contains soft *c* or *g*

_____   _____

5. root contains "id"

_____   _____

6. root ends in "ere"

_____   _____

Challenge

Now challenge your parent to a word search. You go first. Think of one word that fits the first category, and write it down. Then let your parent have a turn. Keep thinking of words for the first category until someone has to pass; then start on category two. See how many words the two of you can come up with.

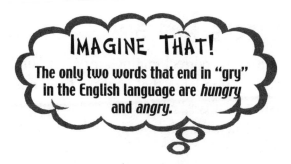

IMAGINE THAT!
The only two words that end in "gry" in the English language are *hungry* and *angry*.

On Your Own

THE GREAT BOOK SEARCH

Search a book you are reading for "ere" words (one point), "id" words (two points), and "ere" or "id" words followed by "ence," "ent," or "ency" (three points). Next, look for "ear" words (one point), "ure" words (two points), and "ear" or "ure" words followed by "ance," "ant," or "ancy" (three points). See how many points you can get.

NEWS SEARCH

Look in the classified section of the newspaper to find something that you would like to buy. Rewrite the ad using as many of the "ance," "ant," "ancy," "ence," "ent," or "ency" words as possible. For example, you might talk about the product's *magnificence, radiance,* or *brilliance.*

CIRCLE AND SAY

Circle the correct endings for each numbered root word and indicate the "ance" or "ence" rule letter that applies. Then make a new word using one of the endings. Not all "a" or "e" endings can always be added to each root word. If you have never heard of the word, don't circle the ending. The first one is done as an example.

The "ance" or "ence" Rules

a. End the word with "ance," "ant," "ancy" after a hard *c* or *g* sound.

b. End the word with "ance," "ant," "ancy" if you can add "ation" to the end of the root.

c. End the word with "ance," "ant," "ancy" if the root ends in "ear" or "ure."

d. End the word with "ence," "ent," "ency" after a soft *c* or *g* sound.

e. End the word with "ence," "ent," "ency" after an "id."

f. End the word with "ence," "ent," "ency" if the root ends in "ere."

Root Word	Ending						Rule	New Word
1. irritate	(ance)	(ant)	(ancy)	ence	ent	ency	b	irritant
2. interfere	ance	ant	ancy	ence	ent	ency		
3. confide	ance	ant	ancy	ence	ent	ency		
4. indulge	ance	ant	ancy	ence	ent	ency		
5. assure	ance	ant	ancy	ence	ent	ency		
6. expect	ance	ant	ancy	ence	ent	ency		

SOFT AND HARD

While driving down the road, challenge your child to this game involving road and advertising signs. Earn one point for each soft *c* or *g* sound-spelling (like *cellular* or *generous*) that you find and three points for each soft *c* or *g* sound followed by "ence," "ent," or "ency." Then switch and earn one point for each hard *c* or *g* sound-spelling (like *cash* or *garage*) and three points for each hard *c* or *g* sound followed by "ance," "ant," or "ancy."

ABLE TO BE INVISIBLE

Parents' Corner

Rule # 14: "able" or "ible"—Use "able" after a hard *c* or hard *g* sound (*applicable, navigable*), to follow a root word—also called a baseword (*readable*), to follow a silent "e" (*changeable*), or if the root can end with "ation" (*irritation/irritable*). End a word with "ible" after a soft *c* or *g* sound (*invincible, eligible*), after an "ss" (*permissible*), or after root word part (*visible*).

The "able" or "ible" rule helps with one of the spelling mistakes that adults make most often. Older students will find this rule particularly helpful because these endings are found in more sophisticated vocabulary.

A root is the part of the word that carries the meaning. For example, in the word *preview,* the root is *view,* and it happens to be a root word. In other cases, the root might be a word part, such as the root "vis" in the word *invisible.* Most of the time, roots that are not complete words are foreign roots.

When adding "able" or "ible" to the end of a word:

If	Then
the root contains hard *c* or *g* sound the root is a complete word the root ends in silent "e"	end in "able"
the root contains soft *c* or *g* sound the root ends in "ss" the root is a word part the root can end in "ation"	end in "ible"

AT THE KITCHEN TABLE

WACKY WORD SORT

Sort the words listed here into the seven categories that follow. Note that some words are listed more than once. List each word under as many categories as apply.

usable	huggable	audible	accessible	eligible	dependable
comparable	applicable	dress	reducible	terrible	laughable

1. hard *c* or *g* sound

2. complete root word

3. soft *c* or *g* sound

4. root word part

5. silent "e"

6. can add "ation"

7. ends in "ss"

Challenge

Now challenge your parent to a word search. You go first. Think of one word that fits the first category, and write it down. Then let your parent have a turn. Keep thinking of words for the first category until someone has to pass; then start on category two. See how many words the two of you can come up with.

On Your Own

IRRESISTIBLE GREETINGS

Make a greeting card for someone special using "able" and "ible" words to describe that lucky person. For example, you might call someone *adorable* or *irresistible*.

SCHOOL BOOK SEARCH

Search your school textbooks for words with roots that end in silent "e" and have "able" endings. Remember that these words follow the Silent "e" Rule (See Rules That Rock: The Sweet Sixteen in chapter 1) when these endings have been added. Also look for roots that end in "ss" and have "ible" endings. See how many you can find in five minutes.

IMAGINE THAT!
The longest word that can be printed without repeating a letter came off the Internet, so surely it's *uncopyrightable.* Count 'em up: 15 letters without a repeat!

CIRCLE AND SAY

Circle the correct ending for each numbered root word and tell the "able" or "ible" rule letters that apply. Then make a new word using the appropriate ending. When the conditions of the "able" or "ible" rule conflict, check the dictionary. The first one is done as an example.

a. End a word with "able" after a hard *c* or *g* sound.
b. End a word with "able" if it follows a complete root word.
c. End a word with "ible" after a soft *c* or *g* sound.
d. End a word with "ible" after a root word part.
e. End a word with "able" if it follows a silent "e."
f. End a word with "able" if the root can end with "ation."
g. End a word with "ible" if the word ends in "ss."

Root Word	Ending		Rules	New Word
1. vis	able	(ible)	d	visible
2. break	able	ible		
3. excuse	able	ible		
4. apply	(c)able	(c)ible		
5. ed	able	ible		
6. adore	able	ible		
7. force	able	ible		
8. leg	able	ible		
9. tug	able	ible		
10. confess	able	ible		

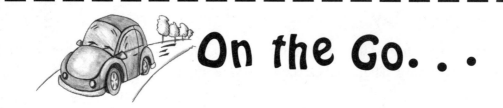

On the Go. . .

ROAD SIGN RACES

Challenge your child to a game of Road Sign Races as you travel to your next activity for the day. Finding words on road or advertising signs, each person earns one point for any soft *c* or *g* sound-spelling (like *celery* or *Germany*) and three points for a soft *c* or *g* sound followed by "ible." After a while, switch so that each player earns one point for any hard *c* or *g* sound-spelling (like *car* or *guest*) and three points for each hard *c* or *g* sound followed by "able."

IS IT AN ILLUSION?

Parents' Corner

Rule #15: "sion," "cian," or "tion"—The final *zyun* sound is usually spelled "sion" (*explosion*). The final *shun* sound is usually spelled "sion" when after an "l" or "s" (*compulsion, passion*), "cian" when the word represents a person (*magician*), and "tion" (*motion*) in most other cases.

Whether to use "sion," "cian," or "tion" is one of the most difficult choices in the English spelling system. Even the best adult speller can get tripped up when spelling these word-ending syllables. Both children and adults have to use the dictionary far more often than is necessary to check spellings of words that end in "sion," "cian," or "tion."

The key to understanding and applying this rule is proper pronunciation. How a word sounds affects its spelling. Provide plenty of examples and listen carefully to your child's pronunciation of the *zyun* sound (with the "sion" spelling) and the *shun* sound (with the "sion," "cian," and "tion" spellings). Proper pronunciation will help your child know when to use each spelling.

TEACHING TIPS

✓ Review the table until your child has memorized the conditions for the "sion," "cian," and "tion" endings.

✓ Help your child to correctly pronounce the *zyun* and *shun* sounds.

✓ Ask your child to give examples of the rule for all conditions.

When deciding which ending to use:

If	Then
The final sound in a word is *zyun* The final sound in a word is *shun* and the root ends in "l" or "s"	End in "sion"
The word represents a person	End in "cian"
Most other cases	End in "tion"

UNSCRAMBLED EGGS

Use the letters in the three scrambled words to write as
many words as possible under the "sion," "cian," or
"tion" headings. You can use any letters from
the three words for the words you create, but
you don't have to use all of the letters. Get one
point for each "sion," "cian," or "tion" correct
spelling and three points for each of the individual
words you unscramble. After you have found a
word, let your parent take a turn. Keep going until
neither player is able to find another word.

nsonfcuoi   hpcaniisy   noatimeigr

"sion"	"cian"	"tion"

MAGAZINE SEARCH

Search magazines for words ending in "sion," "cian," or "tion." Cut each of these words out, and place them in an envelope. Have a parent pick out a word from the envelope and quiz you on how to spell the word and why you spell it that way.

IMAGINE THAT!

In the English language, sounds can be spelled so many different ways. The *sh* sound can be spelled 13 different ways: *shoe, sugar, ocean, issue, nation, fuchsia, schist, pshaw, suspicion, nauseous, conscious, chaperone, mansion.*

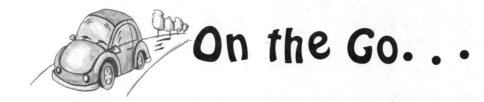

On the Go. . .

WHO CAN SPELL THE LONGEST WORD?

Challenge your child to see who can say and correctly spell the longest "sion," "cian," and "tion" words possible. This one will take a lot of concentration!

ROAD SIGN RACES

Search road or advertising signs for words that have the *zyun* sound. Remember that the *zyun* sound is generally spelled "sion." See who can find the most words.

On Your Own

HIDDEN WORDS

Find and circle the six "sion," "cian," or "tion" words in this word search puzzle. To make things interesting, the words may go horizontally, vertically, or diagonally, and backward or forward.

electrician   musician   mansion   mission   fraction   creation

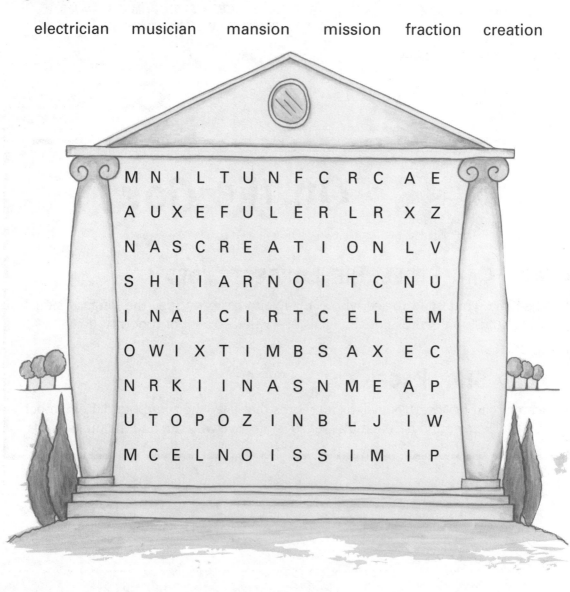

```
M N I L T U N F C R C A E
A U X E F U L E R L R X Z
N A S C R E A T I O N L V
S H I I A R N O I T C N U
I N A I C I R T C E L E M
O W I X T I M B S A X E C
N R K I I N A S N M E A P
U T O P O Z I N B L J I W
M C E L N O I S S I M I P
```

WACKY WORD SORT

Sort the words below into four groups. Seeing these spellings in the different groups will really help you learn to apply this rule.

illusion	musician	vacation	transition	physician
permission	transmission	position	potion	magician
passion	confusion	presentation	beautician	creation
evolution	information	technician	explosion	compulsion
mission	lotion	education	condition	perforation

zyun Sound	"l" or "s" with *shun* Sound	Person	Most Other

WHEN IN DOUBT, GUESS!

Parents' Corner

Rule #16: When in Doubt, Guess!—Unfortunately, the 15 rules addressed in chapters 2, 3 and 4 don't cover all difficult spellings. Even the most consistent of these rules has exceptions. Make sure your child understands that although not all difficult spellings have perfectly consistent rules, memorizing and practicing the rules that work most of the time is still worthwhile. Point out that memorizing some exceptions as spelling sight words is certainly better than memorizing all spelling words as sight words.

Our brains extend learning by applying language generalizations through the process of analogy. The sound-spelling patterns, developed as rules in the Rules That Rock: The Sweet Sixteen, will enable your child to apply these patterns to many of our English words. Your child will become a more consistent speller by learning and using these spelling rules.

Teaching Tips

✓ Help your child memorize the What Works Most list in the first At the Kitchen Table.

✓ When your child finds a word in his or her reading, spelling list, or writing that does not fit rules 1–15, refer to the What Works Most list. Have your child record the word on a Personal Spelling List (see chapter 5).

✓ See chapter 5 for memorization techniques to help your child commit the spelling of the word to memory.

When your child is unsure of how to spell a word not covered by these spelling rules, the first thing he or she should do is look the word up in the dictionary. When this is not practical—as during a test—children need to learn to make educated guesses based on what is most common. The list in the At the Kitchen Table activity is a good source for educated guesses.

AT THE KITCHEN TABLE

MEDIA MANIA

When deciding between two possible endings, refer to the following list to make an educated guess. More often than not, the first of the two possible spellings shown here will be correct.

Think "c," Not "s"
"acy" *(privacy)* instead of "asy" *(fantasy)*
"ce" *(dance)* instead of "se" *(sense)*
"ence" *(presence)* instead of "ense" *(defense)*

Think "i," Not "e"
"ify" *(clarify)* instead of "efy" *(liquefy)*
"ious" *(precious)* instead of "eous" *(courteous)*

And the Rest . . .
"ap" *(apology)* instead of "app" *(apply)*
"aid" *(paid)* instead of "ayed" *(prayed)*
"ary" *(dictionary)* instead of "ery" *(very)* or "ory" *(factory)*
"ope" *(hope)* instead of "oap" *(soap)*
"cede" *(precede)* instead of "ceed" *(succeed)*
"ize" *(realize)* instead of "ise" *(exercise)* or "yze" *(analyze)*

Look in newspapers and magazines to find words with the spellings in the list above. On a separate piece of paper, record the words according to the categories. Score one point for each word that is spelled according to the first of the two possibilities and five points for each word that is not.

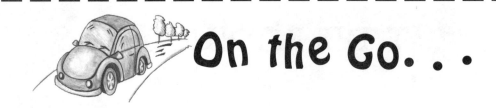

On the Go. . .

SEARCH AND FIND

Find real-world uses on road and advertising signs of What Works Most. Keep track of how many of these words fit the What Works Most rules. When your child sees how often these words do fit the rule, he or she will feel more secure about guessing.

On Your Own

WHAT WORKS MOST?

Find words that fit the rules on page 79 in magazines or newspapers and compose a song to a favorite melody using them.

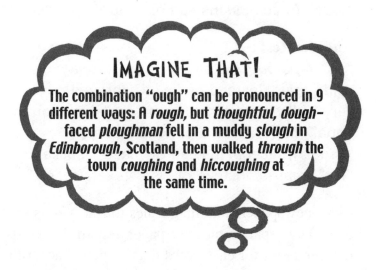

IMAGINE THAT!

The combination "ough" can be pronounced in 9 different ways: A *rough,* but *thoughtful, dough-*faced *ploughman* fell in a muddy *slough* in *Edinborough,* Scotland, then walked *through* the town *coughing* and *hiccoughing* at the same time.

Chapter 5

The Super Spelling Study Plan

In This Chapter

- To Study or Not to Study

- Keeping Track of the Tough Stuff

- Tricks to Memorize By

- Pick a Pack of Study Cards

- You Mean I Have to Use My Brain?

TO STUDY OR NOT TO STUDY

Parents' Corner

All too often, students spend too much time studying what they already know and too little time studying what they don't know. If your child gets half of the weekly spelling words correct on the Monday pretest, the rest of the week should be spent studying *only* the weekly spelling words that he or she does not know how to spell.

Instead of having your child practice the weekly spelling words he or she already knows in workbook exercises, it would be better to help your child find and practice unknown words and spelling patterns. The Magic 30 Spelling Test in chapter 1 is an excellent source to help you decide which of the Rules That Rock: The Sweet Sixteen your child needs to learn. In addition, the appendices provide lists of the spelling words that are the most important for your intermediate-age child to master.

TEACHING TIPS

✓ If your child's teacher gives a spelling pretest, ask your child to bring home the corrected test as a starting point.

✓ Give your child a spelling pretest from not yet mastered spelling pattern words in chapters 2, 3, and 4 and the appendices word lists.

✓ Continue the test up to the point where your child has missed enough words to supplement any spelling pretest errors.

The Super Spelling Plan will help you develop an individualized weekly spelling list of the words that are most appropriate for your child to study and practice. The plan is designed either to supplement the weekly list of words from your child's school spelling program or to be used on its own, apart from the classroom, in a homeschool situation. This plan will help your child learn how to study, memorize, practice, and retain the spelling words.

WEEKLY WORDS

With your parent, create a list of weekly spelling words that you don't already know how to spell. If you take a spelling pretest at school, bring home the corrected test and write down any spelling words you missed on your Personal Spelling List (see the next lesson). Don't include the words that you spelled correctly, because you already know those spellings. Add to the list any words that you misspelled in your weekly writing assignments and any words missed on last week's spelling post-test. If you don't have a weekly spelling list, you will be creating your own list.

Have your parent test you on words from the appendices of this book or from the spelling patterns that you are working on in chapters 2, 3, and 4. Print each of the words in pencil on binder paper. After each word that your parent dictates, have your parent say each letter of the spelling so that you can self-correct.

Mark a dot on top of each correct letter as your parent says each letter. If you miss a letter or add a letter that shouldn't be in the word, place an "X" through the word and print the word correctly next to your spelling mistake. Have your parent check your corrected spellings. Continue taking the test until you find enough words that you don't know how to spell so that you can complete the 20 words on your Personal Spelling List.

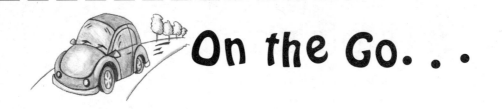

On the Go. . .

PARENT TOUGHIES

Here's news that your child probably already figured out . . . parents don't know everything! Think of the five words that you have the hardest time spelling. Spell them out loud (to the best of your ability) while your child writes them down. Then have your child look up the words in the dictionary to check the spellings. Add these words to the week's Personal Spelling List.

On Your Own

COLLECT OR REJECT

Be a word collector! From the Rules That Rock: The Sweet Sixteen, pick any spelling pattern that is challenging for you (see chapters 2–4). Then, search the newspaper or your favorite magazine to find as many words that fit that spelling pattern as you can. Use these words to help fill up the week's Personal Spelling List. Don't pick any words that you already know how to spell.

IMAGINE THAT!

America is named after Italian explorer Emerigo Vespucci, *sideburns* is named after Northern Civil War general Ambrose Burnside who had bushy whiskers, and *sandwich* is named after the Fourth Earl of Sandwich, who invented this food so he could gamble while eating.

KEEPING TRACK OF THE TOUGH STUFF

Parents' Corner

Researchers say that spellers make most of their mistakes from a group of about 40 common words specific to each speller. Making a Personal Spelling List of problematic words will help your child keep track of these words. This list will help your child work with problem words and will also be a wonderful mini-spelling dictionary for reference.

In addition to keeping track of difficult words, the Personal Spelling List is designed to help your child effectively study these words. It is important to have your child print each spelling word accurately and neatly under the Correct Word column. Make sure you check these spellings, because children often copy words incorrectly.

TEACHING TIPS

✓ Make enough copies of the Personal Spelling List for one list per week of instruction.

✓ Tell your child to carefully print each spelling word in the Correct Word column.

✓ Have your child print how he or she misspelled each word in the How Misspelled column. Have your child circle any misspelled letters in the How Misspelled words.

✓ Help your child identify words that are spelling patterns addressed in the Rules That Rock: The Sweet Sixteen. Briefly summarize the relevant part of the rule in the Rule Reminder column.

The How Misspelled column will help your child identify what part of the spelling word created difficulties. Your child should copy the word the way it was misspelled on the test or writing assignment and then circle the problem letters or section of the word that caused the misspelling. Isolating the spelling problem will help your child identify any spelling rules that pertain to the misspelling. If there is a rule that relates, it should be briefly summarized under the Rule Reminder column.

By identifying how the word was misspelled, your child will also be able to devise a memory reminder under the Memory Keys, Word Clues, Pict-o-Words column.

AT THE KITCHEN TABLE

PERSONAL SPELLING LIST

This activity will provide you with your own personal spelling list. Before you begin, copy the column heads below into a notebook that you will use as your weekly spelling list book.

Personal Spelling List

Correct Word	How Misspelled	Rule Reminder	Memory Keys, Word Clues, Pict-o-Words

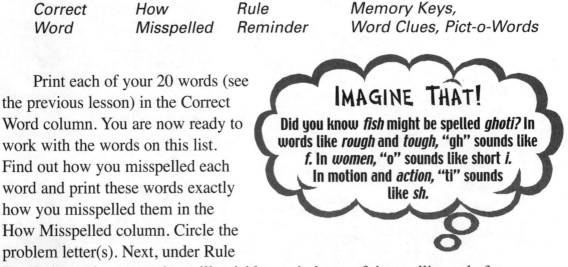

IMAGINE THAT!

Did you know *fish* might be spelled *ghoti?* In words like *rough* and *tough,* "gh" sounds like *f.* In *women,* "o" sounds like short *i.* In motion and *action,* "ti" sounds like *sh.*

Print each of your 20 words (see the previous lesson) in the Correct Word column. You are now ready to work with the words on this list. Find out how you misspelled each word and print these words exactly how you misspelled them in the How Misspelled column. Circle the problem letter(s). Next, under Rule Reminder, write a note that will quickly remind you of the spelling rule from chapter 2, 3, or 4. If there is no spelling rule that helps explain the correct spelling of the word, just leave the Rule Reminder blank for that word. Here's an example:

Correct Word	How Misspelled	Rule Reminder	Memory Keys, Word Clues, Pict-o-Words
thier	their	"i" before "e"	

For now, leave the last column blank. You'll learn more about Memory Keys, Word Clues, and Pict-o-Words in the next lesson.

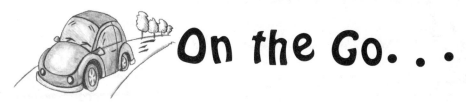

On the Go. . .

SPELLING CHAMELEON

While running errands, work with your child to change the form of each of the words from the weekly spelling list. Your child can switch the verb tense, make a singular noun into a plural, add a prefix or a suffix, and so on. Alternate saying and spelling the new forms of the words. Here's an example:

> **Parent:** The word is "infect."
> **Child:** Infected.
> **Parent:** i-n-f-e-c-t-e-d.

Now it's your child's turn to come up with word.

On Your Own

HUNTING DOWN MISTAKES

Go on a spelling mistake hunt. Spelling mistakes are everywhere. Sometimes people make mistakes on purpose to get your attention. For example, Toys "R" Us has the "R" placed backward to appeal to children. Look for misspelled words in magazine articles, fast-food signs, e-mails, or just about anywhere. Try to determine whether the spelling error was made on purpose.

TRICKS TO MEMORIZE BY

Parents' Corner

We all remember things best when we can relate the unknown to the known. We also remember information that is recent, repeated, exciting, interesting, or even embarrassing. Unless we make an effort to make the unknown memorable when it is first learned, it will soon be forgotten. This is true with remembering difficult spelling words.

Even though your child may not have a "photographic" memory, he or she can develop a better spelling memory. Students can learn to memorize and apply spelling patterns to similar words. Memory Keys, Word Clues, and Pict-o-Words are three memory association techniques that can help your child remember how to spell difficult words.

Memory Keys are associations that help you remember the spelling of difficult words by relating words or ideas to confusing letter combinations. Word Clues have been used throughout the ages to connect the unknown (the problem spelling word) with the known (a word within the difficult spelling word that will help you remember how to spell the word). Pict-o-Words help you remember difficult spellings by identifying key letter combinations and then creating a picture to focus the memory on the problem areas. Any of these memory association techniques can be included on the Personal Spelling List under the Memory Keys, Word Clues, Pict-o-Words column.

TEACHING TIPS

✓ Have your child select difficult words from the Personal Spelling List that do not conform to the spelling patterns in the Rules That Rock: The Sweet Sixteen.

✓ Teach your child to connect these letter combinations to related words or ideas called Memory Keys.

✓ Explain how to use Word Clues (a smaller word within the difficult spelling word that has the same letter combinations that cause the spelling mistake).

✓ Show your child how to draw Pict-o-Words to visually represent difficult letter combinations.

AT THE KITCHEN TABLE

MEMORY KEYS

Sometimes, you can use associations to help you remember difficult things, like spellings. Memory Keys are a kind of association in which you relate words or ideas to difficult letter combinations to help you remember the spelling of difficult words. Here are some examples:

Spelling Problem: How do you know when to spell *desert* or *dessert?*

Correct Word: dessert

How Misspelled: desert

Memory Key: More de**ss**ert (with two of the letter "s") is definitely better than more de**s**ert (with only one of the letter "s").

Pick three words from the following word list and develop Memory Keys for each.

presume	slowly	miscellaneous	highly	blue
checking	preview	filibuster	struck	carefully
prefix	partly	clique	tart	sticker
bun	precipitate	seriously	prevaricate	clueless

Word   **Memory Key Clue**

1. _____ _____

2. _____ _____

3. _____ _____

WORD CLUES

Word Clues are another memory trick to help you memorize difficult spellings. Word Clues connect the unknown (a problem spelling word) with the known (a word within the difficult spelling word that will help you remember how to spell the word).

Spelling Problem: Is the spelling argument or arguement?
Correct Word: argument
How Misspelled: arguement
Word Clue: gum; "Ar<u>gum</u>ents are worth chewing on." There is no "e" between the "u" and the "m."

Now pick three words from the list on page 89 and develop Word Clues for them.

Word	Word Clue
1. _____	_____
2. _____	_____
3. _____	_____

PICT-O-WORDS

Pict-o-words are illustrations of difficult letter combinations that will help you remember how to spell certain words. Here is an example:

Spelling Problem: wagon; How can you remember that the second vowel is an "o"? This ə sound could be spelled with any vowel, so this word is difficult.

Correct Word: wagon

How Misspelled: wagun, wagen, wagin, wagan

Pict-o-Word: The wagon wheel in the letter "o" helps you remember that the word is spelled with an "o" and not any other vowel. A wagon wheel inside of any other vowel sure would create a bumpy ride!

Now pick three words from the list on page 89. Develop Pict-o-Word clues for each word—the simpler the drawing, the better. First, choose the difficult letter combinations for each word. Then, think of another word, or a part of a word, that you know how to spell that includes the same difficult letter combinations. Include this word as part of your drawing.

Word	Pict-o-Word Clue
1. _____	
2. _____	
3. _____	

On the Go. . .

LITTLE WITHIN BIG

Memory Keys, Word Clues, and Pict-o-Words each associate words your child knows with words that are difficult for your child to spell. One great way to practice these associations is to find little, easy-to-spell words that are hiding in bigger, more difficult-to-spell words. Use billboards and road signs to find little words within big ones. You might find *rest* within *restaurant*, *mob* within *automobile*, or *deli* within *indelible*. Find ways to use these little words to remember the bigger words. For example, when you eat at a restaurant, you take a *rest* from cooking at home. Or imagine a *mob* of people crammed into an automobile.

On Your Own

BRAINSTORM

Brainstorm and draw Memory Keys, Word Clues, or Pict-o-Words for the words on your Personal Spelling List that don't have any spelling patterns written in the Rule Reminder column. Be creative!

IMAGINE THAT!

Knowing how to spell some words really helps us know how to spell others. *Insignia* may be difficult to spell, but not when you notice the *sign* within it. *Nationality* gives most people fits, but not if they notice the word *nation* tucked inside.

PICK A PACK OF STUDY CARDS

Parents' Corner

Making study cards can be key to your child's spelling success. The activity of printing out the spelling words listed on the weekly Personal Spelling List helps with retention. Sorting the cards into similar groups for study helps your child memorize better, because people tend to remember information learned in visual patterns. This is not to say that studying the way a word is shaped is helpful, but rather that it is worthwhile to study how the spelling features of a word compare with other words. Have your child sort spelling patterns in this order:

TEACHING TIPS

✓ Have your child print each spelling word for his or her weekly spelling list on a separate 3 × 5 card.

✓ Check each spelling to make sure your child will be studying correctly spelled words.

✓ Have your child lay out the spelling study cards and sort them into similar groups.

✓ Explain that there may be cards that won't fit into groups.

1. Sort by similar prefixes (if any).

2. Sort next by similar suffixes (if any).

3. Sort by similar vowel patterns (if any).

4. Sort by similar consonant patterns (if any).

5. Sort by similar word lengths (if any) or as exceptions to the other groups.

6. Sort out the spelling words that are quickly mastered from the ones that need more practice.

Make sure your child prints each card neatly and accurately. Students sometimes can't read their own writing when they are sloppy. Once a child has studied and learned the wrong spelling of a word, he or she will have a hard time replacing it with the correct spelling in his or her memory.

AT THE KiTCHEN TABLE

SORT AND SPELL

Studying spelling words in similar word groups will help you memorize better. Look at this list of weekly spelling words.

presume	slowly	miscellaneous	highly	blue
checking	preview	filibuster	struck	carefully
prefix	partly	clique	tart	sticker
bun	precipitate	seriously	prevaricate	clueless

Sort the words into the following categories. After you have used a word once, cross it off your list and do not use it again.

1. Make a group of words with similar prefixes.

_____

_____

2. Make a group of words with similar suffixes.

_____

_____

3. Make a group of words with the same vowel cluster patterns.

_____

_____

4. Make a group of words with similar consonant cluster patterns.

_____

_____

5. Make another group by words with similar consonant cluster patterns.

_____

_____

6. Make groups of words by similar length. Then list any leftover words.

_____

_____

On Your Own

Solo Word Sort

Ask your parent for some 3 × 5 index cards or some old business cards. Carefully print each word from your Personal Spelling List on a different card. Sort these spelling study cards into the same categories used in the At the Kitchen Table

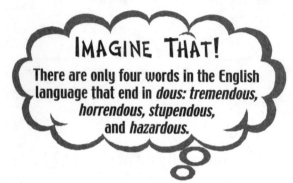

IMAGINE THAT!

There are only four words in the English language that end in *dous: tremendous, horrendous, stupendous,* and *hazardous.*

activity earlier in this lesson. There are probably some words that don't fit into any of the categories. Put these words at the back of your cards when you stack them together. Studying these spelling study cards in this order will really help you remember each spelling.

On the Go. . .

Word Sort Switcheroo

Pick one of the Word Sort Categories and ask your child to find as many words that fit the category in a set amount of time. If you're at the doctor's office, flip through magazines. If you're in the grocery store, look at food packaging, and so on. Then, switch roles: Your child picks the category, and you find the words that fit.

YOU MEAN I HAVE TO USE MY BRAIN?

Parents' Corner

Recent brain research has raised some interesting issues regarding memory. Researchers have found that a physical stimulus can more actively engage a particular brain hemisphere. The right hemisphere of the brain stores visual memory. Researchers have also noted that people with the best visual memories look up and to the left with their eyes opened when trying to recall information. Less successful memorizers tend to look down during recall. (Remember that the right side of the brain controls the left side of the body.)

These findings have led to a theoretical application for studying spelling. When a person looks up and to the left when memorizing the visual picture and letter relationships of a word, the eyes actually see a mirror image of the word, stimulating the right side of the brain. To assist in visualizing this picture of the word, it is helpful to recite the letters backward and out loud. Visualizing and practicing the letters backward helps your child focus on the sequence of letter relationships and makes the spelling of the word more memorable. Whether or not further research confirms this technique as a sound teaching/study practice, it is a highly motivating and fun way to memorize difficult spelling words. Note that children seem to do much better with this study technique than do adults.

TEACHING TIPS

✓ Have your child select his or her most difficult spelling words from the pack of study cards.

✓ Work through the At the Kitchen Table activity with your child after he or she has read the directions.

✓ Remind your child that this is just one study technique to use with the spelling study cards.

AT THE KITCHEN TABLE

MEMORY TECHNIQUE

Read the following instructions before you begin this activity. Then have a parent read them to you to remind you of the steps as you do the activity.

Sort out a group of five of your more difficult spelling study cards. Hold one of these cards slightly up and to the left of your head so that your eyes look up and to the left. Now form a mental image of the word, noting the order of the letters and preparing to spell the word backward.

Drop the card, but keep your eyes open, looking up and to the left. Spell the word backward. If you begin to stumble or miss a letter, refresh your memory by picking up the card looking up and to the left at it again. Continue until you have spelled the word backward correctly.

Check the word by looking up and to the left again. Reform the mental image to prepare to spell the word forward. Now drop the card, but keep your eyes open, looking up and to the left. Spell the word forward. If you begin to stumble or miss a letter, refresh your memory by looking up and to the left at the card again. Continue until you have spelled the word forward correctly.

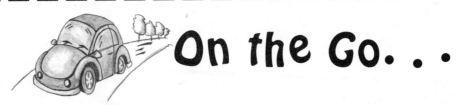

On the Go...

THE TOUGH ONES

Pick difficult words from your child's spelling list or any difficult words from magazine advertisements or something similar. Spell the word backward twice, and then have your child say the word and spell it forward correctly. Here's an example:

Parent: g-n-i-l-l-e-p-s—g-n-i-l-l-e-p-s—What's the name of the spelling word?

Child: spelling—s-p-e-l-l-i-n-g

On Your Own

PUT 'EM UP!

Practice spelling all of your Personal Spelling List words using the up-and-to-the-left memory technique that you practiced in the At the Kitchen Table activity. You will find that this method of studying really helps you see the whole word and remember difficult letter combinations. Also, it's a lot of fun!

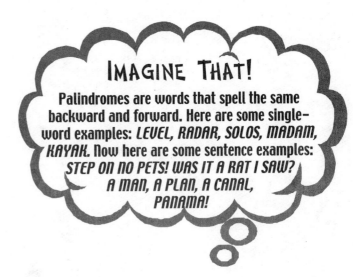

IMAGINE THAT!

Palindromes are words that spell the same backward and forward. Here are some single-word examples: *LEVEL, RADAR, SOLOS, MADAM, KAYAK.* Now here are some sentence examples: *STEP ON NO PETS! WAS IT A RAT I SAW? A MAN, A PLAN, A CANAL, PANAMA!*

Chapter 6

Get It? Write
the First Time

In This Chapter

- Sound-Spelling Patterns: Spelling Problem-Solving

- Poofreading Catches 50 Percent of Selling Errors

- Spell-Check: The Thing in My Pea See

SOUND-SPELLING PATTERNS: SPELLING PROBLEM-SOLVING

Parents' Corner

The Sound-Spellings Chart gives you the tools to teach spelling where it counts the most—in writing. After all, your child won't be taking spelling tests throughout life, but he or she *will* be writing. This chart provides the most common of the 256 different spellings of English speech sounds. By using this chart, your child will learn how to apply problem-solving spelling strategies in writing assignments.

The Sound-Spellings Chart will give your child the spelling patterns that are most often used for each speech sound. With a few key teaching strategies, you will be able to help your child learn how to narrow down possible spellings of difficult words, and so to write fluently—without constantly checking spellings with the dictionary, the spell-checker, or an adult.

The Sound-Spellings Chart shows the individual sounds that are pronounced in words under the Sound column and the most commonly used spellings for each sound under the Spellings column. The blanks in the Spellings column mean that other letters must go in those blanks. For example, in the "__ck" spelling, "ck" can never start any syllable or word; "ck" can only be spelled at the end of a syllable or word, such as in the word *check*. This is an important concept for your child to develop as he or she learns to strategically choose among spelling options.

TEACHING TIPS

✓ Review how The Sound-Spellings Chart is organized, explaining the difference between consonants and vowels and short and long vowel marks, if necessary.

✓ Explain that the spelling blanks in the Spellings column on The Sound-Spellings Chart mean that other letters must go in those blanks.

✓ Check out Prima Publishing's *Better Phonics and Beyond in 5 Minutes a Day* to help your child master the sound-spelling relationships.

AT THE KITCHEN TABLE

THE SOUND-SPELLING CHART CHALLENGE

Refer to The Sound-Spellings Chart in this section to answer The Sound-Spelling Chart Challenge questions. Be sure to use The Sound-Spellings Chart to check and correct spelling errors in your writing.

1. How many consonant sounds have three different spellings each?

2. Which short vowel sound can be spelled with "a," "e," "i," "o," and "u"?

3. How many sounds do you hear when you pronounce each of the consonant pair spellings?

4. What has to go in the blanks in the Spelling column? (These are called "spelling blanks.")

5. What real spelling word could be misspelled "dgeump" if someone didn't understand how spelling blanks work?

6. Name the two different sounds that the letter "y" can have at the end of a syllable or word.

7. What long vowel sound has the most spellings?

8. What other vowel spellings can only come at the end of a syllable or word?

The Sound-Spellings Chart

Consonant Spellings

Sound	Spellings	Sample Words
b	b	bat
k	c, k, __ck	cat, kitchen, luck
d	d	dot
f	f, ph	fox, phone
g	g	gecko
h	h__	hen
j	j__, g, __dge	jam, gel, edge

Note: "g" before "e," "i," "y"; "__dge" with short vowels

Sound	Spellings	Sample Words
kw	qu__	quarter
l	l	lake
m	m	mom
n	n, kn__, gn	nose, knife, gnome
p	p	potato
er	r, wr__	rat, wren
s	s, ce, ci__, cy	seat, celery, Cindy, cycle
t	t	top
v	v	van
w	w	wig
ks	__x	box
y	y__	yellow
z	z, __s	zebra, hoses
zh	__s__	measure
ch	ch, __tch	chimp, match

Consonant Team Spellings

Sound	Spellings	Sample Words
sh	sh, __ti__, __ci__, __si__	ship, lotion, musician, mansion
th (unvoiced)	th	teeth
th (voiced)	th	them
wh	wh__	whip
ng	__ng	ring

Short Vowel Spellings

Sound	Spellings	Sample Words
ă	a__, au__	cat, laugh
ĕ	e__, __ie__, __ea__	men, friend, bread
ĭ	i__	pig
ŏ	o__, __ou__	box, cough
ŭ	u__, a__, e__, i__, o__	hug, about, started, territory, wagon

Note: The ŭ sound frequently appears in unaccented syllables with any of the above spellings.

Long Vowel Spellings

Sound	Spellings	Sample Words
ā	a, ai__, __ay, ei__, a__e	cradle, rain, bay, sleigh, cake
ē	e, ee, ea, __y, __i__, __ie, e__e	below, seed, bead, baby, marine, chief, complete

Note: The long e "__y" spelling is usually at the end of an unaccented syllable.

Sound	Spellings	Sample Words
ī	i, __igh, __y, __ui__, i__e	pilot, night, try, guide, kite

Note: The long i "__y" spelling is usually at the end of an accented syllable.

Sound	Spellings	Sample Words
ō	o, oa__, ow, o__e	Ohio, oak, owner, code
ū	u, ew, u__e	music, few, huge

Other Vowel Sound Spellings

Sound	Spellings	Sample Words
o͞o	__oo, u, __ue, ew, u__e	boot, duty, glue, stew, dude
ur	ear, er, ir, ur	learn, sister, bird, burn
ar	ar	car
or	or	fork
ow	__ow, ou__	cow, trout
aw	aw, au__, a	hawk, author, ball
oy	oi__, __oy	soil, toy
o͝o	oo, __u__	book, pudding

On the Go...

THIS-A-WAY AND THAT-A-WAY

Pick a sound with multiple spellings from The Sound-Spellings Chart. Challenge your child to look for as many spellings of the same sound as possible on road signs, on advertising signs, in magazines, in comics, or even on packaging at the grocery store.

SOUND GAME

Make a sound, and have your child think of as many ways as possible to spell the sound. Check your answers against The Sound-Spellings Chart.

On Your Own

CHECK IT OUT

Use The Sound-Spellings Chart to check and correct the errors in this student's spelling test. Write the correct spelling in the space provided.

1. payne _____

2. chekers _____

3. leep _____

4. elefant _____

5. lite _____

6. lege _____

7. nife _____

8. flote _____

9. rite _____

10. burd _____

POOFREADING CATCHES
50 PERCENT OF SELLING ERRORS

Parents' Corner

Up to 50 percent of all spelling errors in writing can be corrected with effective proofreading skills. But wait a minute, you might say, "If my child knew how to spell the word, he or she would!" This is not necessarily true. Many times the child writes carelessly or is so busy concentrating on what to say that he or she makes mistakes.

The proofreading skills taught in this lesson can reduce the amount of careless spelling errors that your child makes in his or her writing. Of course, it is important to proofread for things other than spelling, such as word choice, grammar, punctuation, and overall meaning. But it is best to proofread spelling separately.

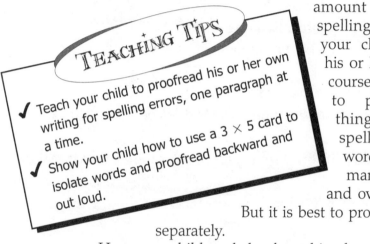

TEACHING TIPS

✓ Teach your child to proofread his or her own writing for spelling errors, one paragraph at a time.

✓ Show your child how to use a 3 × 5 card to isolate words and proofread backward and out loud.

Have your child read aloud anything he or she has written. Correct pronunciation is often an excellent clue to accurate spelling. For example, students frequently misspell the words *I'll* and *probably* because of poor pronunciation: *"All probly* go to the park today." Many times students will correct their own misspellings after correctly pronouncing the misspelled words.

Also, show your child how to use a 3 × 5 card to isolate each word and read each paragraph backward. Children frequently read through incorrect spellings because they are reading for meaning and not thinking about each letter. Reading backward helps to focus on spelling and prohibits reading through the words. For example, reading "today park the to go probly All" focuses attention on the individual words.

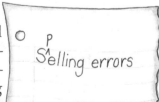

AT THE KITCHEN TABLE

THREE LITTLE PEEGZ?

The child who wrote this start to a familiar story really has some spelling difficulties. First, read silently and try to figure out the individual words from such terrible spellings. Then read out loud to see how much easier it is to understand the words. Reading out loud is an important part of effective proofreading. Now write the correct spellings above each word.

Wunts ah pawn ah tyem, dare wur deez tree leddel peegz zat lift en dah

zaym playz. Eggsulee, day lift en dare owen homz en dah viludg. Wun

uv deez howz s wuz mayd uv ster aw, uhnudder ov stah ix, weth dah

vest wun billt owd uv ber ix.

   Wun mornen, de viludg wulf kaym dew balow dez peegz howz s

dowen. De furest wunz kaym dowen eze, bud de ber ik howz wud ant

fahel. De dum wulf klhimd uhp awn de ruf ant juppd dowen dah cha

emne. Dah tree leddel peegz hadah boyleenk pahot waytink en de

fierplaz. Da wulf fel en de pahot ant de peegz ade im fer lahunj.

V N

ERROR PROOF

Practice proofreading while you and your child are out and about. Look for spelling mistakes on billboards or signs. Unfortunately, there are plenty of these around such as the PED XING (pedestrian crossing) sign right before the cross-walk at your child's school. Say any errors that you find out loud the way the word should be pronounced. Then have your child spell it correctly.

On Your Own

MARY AND THE SPOOKY HOUSE

This author really needs help proofreading. First, silently read through the story and place a dot above each misspelled word. Then, using a 3 × 5 card to isolate each word, read the story backward and out loud to see how many *more* spelling errors you find. Correct the spelling of each word above each misspelling. Reading out loud and backward really makes spelling errors stand out.

Late every nite, Mary Piper set out on a long and familar walk around

her nieghborhood. She past the old elementery school, waived at Mrs.

Walters, who was turning on her pourch light, and then crossed the

drivway of the fire station. Nothing seemed out of the ordinary on that

deep, dark nite in Feburary of 1999.

At the corner of 3rd and Elm, Mary thought she herd a soft, wailing cry down the street. Turning off her usaul path, she began walking down Elm Street to investagate. This was a decision that she would latter regret.

Elm Street was in an older secction of town. It's tall trees swayed in the moonlight and cast taller shadows aginst the two-story homes lineing the street. Not a soul was to be scene or herd. Mary slowed her walk and tried to convince her self that the soft, wailing cry was only the sound of the wind threw the trees. She begun to turn around for home, when a louder cry pierced the night. Mary stopped, dead in her traks.

The sounde seemed to came from the top story of the house at the end of the street. Mary wheeled around, and then brokd into a run.

Mary did not slow to a walk until her feet toutched her front lawn. She

slept pourly that nite, tossing and turning until dawn.

That mourning, Mary read in the newspaper that the very house at

the end of Elm Street that so frightened her the nite before was being

torn down in order to conect Elm Street to the center of town. Perhaps

the wailing sounde that Mary herd was the

house's last wailing cry about leeving Elm

Street forever.

Just for Fun!
What has eight letters
but no letters in it?
An envelope.

SPELL-CHECK: THE THING IN MY PEA SEE

Parents' Corner

Spell checkers can be a wonderful help for anyone using a word processor, and children need to learn how to use this tool. Many times, however, spell checkers actually slow the production of correct final drafts because people over-rely on this tool. These programs frequently miss *homophones* (words that are spelled differently but sound the same) and fail to catch omitted words, for example.

To improve the accuracy and speed of a spelling check, you can set spelling options on a word processing program. For example, in Microsoft Word, if you click on the Tools window and then on Options you will be able to customize the spell checker. You might have the spelling corrected automatically as you type or prefer to have the computer suggest spelling options before you change spellings. Or you may wish to add special dictionaries to your spell checker. The word processing program may have these files ready to activate under the Tools menu or you may need to purchase these.

Teaching Tips

✔ These exercises are intended to point out the types of mistakes commonly overlooked by spell checkers.

✔ If your child has access to a computer, have him or her experiment with word processing and spell checkers.

✔ Teach your child that spell checkers either suggest the best alternative spelling or require you to choose among words that are similar.

Other handheld spell-checkers can also be useful. You can type in your best spelling guess and see the spelling options with a scroll-down feature. Or you can type in the sentence to give the computer some of the grammatical structure to help it suggest a correct spelling. These tools are portable and very helpful, but they do have the same limitations as the full-scale word processing programs. In conclusion, even with the help of spell checkers, effective proofreading is always absolutely necessary.

AT THE KITCHEN TABLE

MY E-MALE

Edit the following poem by writing the correct spellings above each line. Note that a spell checker would not find any errors in this poem.

Eye no sum won named Spell Check.

He lives in my Pea See.

He's awl weighs their to try and help

When I hit a wrong key.

But when I rite an e-male,

On him I can't depend.

I kneed two also proof reed

Bee four I push the SEND.

☀ On Your Own ☀

THE E-MAIL I WISH I HADN'T SENT

Edit the following e-mail by writing the correct spellings above each line.

Dear Martha,

I'm so sad about what has happened to you! I've never seen such a

huge waist, but their loss will be your gain. At least now I'll get to see

more of you. Remember, good things come

to those who weight.

Your Friend, Through Thick and Thin,

John

P.S. Cheer up. You'll find another job soon.

Just for Fun!

Why is the letter "a" so much like a flower?
Because a bee comes after it.

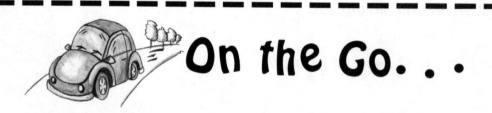

On the Go. . .

HOMOPHONE TAG

Find any word on a road sign, billboard, or advertisement that has a matching homophone. Say the word and then use the matching homophone in a sentence. For example, "*bare:* That *bear* sure likes honey." Then, your child is tagged "it" and must find the next homophone. The last one to find a matching homophone before you reach your destination is the winner. (Homophones are words that sound alike, but are spelled differently and have different meanings.)

The 700 Most Frequently Used Words

Mastering the spelling words that appear most often in intermediate-level reading makes sense. The 700 Most Frequently Used Words are listed in the order in which they most often appear in children's reading texts. These are the words your child will read and write most often. The first 20 of these words make up 25 percent of the most frequently written words in elementary reading books. The first 100 make up 50 percent, and all 700 together make up about 75 percent of a child's elementary reading vocabulary.

When choosing from these words for your child's spelling list, skim through and select only the words that you think your child might misspell. Most intermediate-age children will have the first half of this list already mastered.

After you test your child with the words you choose, have your child add each word missed to his or her Personal Spelling List. When you read through your child's writing assignments from school, pay special attention to any words that your child uses that are also on this list. If you notice any misspellings, make sure to add these words to the Personal Spelling List.

the	an	now	right
of	which	people	look
and	their	my	think
a	said	made	also
to	if	over	around
in	do	did	another
is	will	down	came
you	each	only	come
that	about	way	work
it	how	find	three
he	up	use	must
for	out	may	because
was	them	water	does
on	then	long	part
are	she	little	even
as	many	very	place
with	some	after	well
his	so	words	such
they	these	called	here
at	would	just	take
be	other	where	why
this	into	most	help
from	has	know	put
I	more	get	different
have	her	through	away
or	two	back	again
by	like	much	off
one	him	go	went
had	see	good	old
not	time	new	number
but	could	write	great
what	no	our	tell
all	make	me	men
were	than	man	say
when	first	too	small
we	been	any	every
there	its	day	found
can	who	same	still

between	going	let	against
name	want	night	top
should	school	picture	turned
home	important	being	learn
big	until	study	point
give	form	second	city
air	food	soon	play
line	keep	story	toward
set	children	since	five
own	feet	white	himself
under	land	ever	usually
read	side	paper	money
last	without	hard	seen
never	boy	near	didn't
us	once	sentence	car
left	animal	better	morning
end	life	best	I'm
along	enough	across	body
while	took	during	upon
might	four	today	family
next	head	however	later
sound	above	sure	turn
below	kind	knew	move
saw	began	it's	face
something	almost	try	door
thought	live	told	cut
both	page	young	done
few	got	sun	group
those	earth	thing	true
always	need	whole	half
show	far	hear	red
large	hand	example	fish
often	high	heard	plants
together	year	several	living
asked	mother	change	black
house	light	answer	eat
don't	country	room	short
world	father	sea	United States

run	letter	area	problem
book	among	horse	longer
gave	able	matter	winter
order	dog	stand	deep
open	shown	box	heavy
ground	mean	start	carefully
cold	English	that's	follow
really	rest	class	beautiful
table	perhaps	piece	everyone
remember	certain	surface	leave
tree	six	river	everything
course	feel	common	game
front	fire	stop	system
American	ready	am	bring
space	green	talk	watch
inside	yes	whether	shell
ago	built	fine	dry
sad	ran	round	within
early	full	dark	floor
I'll	town	past	ice
learned	complete	ball	ship
brought	oh	girl	themselves
close	hot	road	begin
nothing	anything	blue	fact
though	hold	instead	third
idea	state	either	quite
before	list	held	carry
lived	stood	already	distance
became	hundred	warm	although
add	ten	gone	sat
become	fast	finally	possible
grow	felt	summer	heart
draw	kept	understand	real
yet	notice	moon	simple
less	can't	animals	snow
wind	strong	mind	rain
behind	voice	outside	suddenly
cannot	probably	power	easy

leaves	friend	thus	soil
lay	language	square	human
size	job	moment	trip
wild	music	teacher	woman
weather	buy	happy	eye
miss	window	bright	milk
pattern	mark	sent	choose
sky	heat	present	north
walked	grew	plan	seven
main	listen	rather	famous
someone	ask	length	late
center	single	speed	pay
field	clear	machine	sleep
stay	energy	information	iron
itself	week	except	trouble
boat	explain	figure	store
question	lost	you're	beside
wide	spring	free	oil
least	travel	fell	modern
tiny	wrote	suppose	fun
hour	farm	natural	catch
happened	circle	ocean	business
foot	whose	government	reach
care	correct	baby	lot
low	bed	grass	won't
else	measure	plane	case
gold	straight	street	speak
build	base	couldn't	shape
glass	mountain	reason	eight
rock	caught	difference	edge
tall	hair	maybe	soft
alone	bird	history	village
bottom	wood	mouth	object
check	color	middle	age
reading	war	step	minute
fall	fly	child	wall
poor	yourself	strange	meet
map	seem	wish	record

copy	sand	garden	anyone
forest	tail	led	rule
especially	wait	note	science
necessary	difficult	various	afraid
he's	general	race	women
unit	cover	bit	produce
flat	material	result	pull
direction	isn't	brother	son
south	thousand	addition	meant
subject	sign	doesn't	broken
skin	guess	dead	interest
wasn't	forward	weight	chance
I've	huge	thin	thick
yellow	ride	stone	sight
party	region	hit	pretty
force	nor	wife	train
test	period	island	fresh
bad	blood	we'll	drive
temperature	rich	opposite	lead
pair	team	born	break
ahead	corner	sense	
wrong	cat	cattle	
practice	amount	million	

Appendix B

120 Elementary Spelling Toughies

Even adults have a few words that they have trouble spelling. The following list of 120 Elementary Spelling Toughies has been compiled over the years from student writing in the intermediate grades.

When choosing from this list for your child's weekly spelling list, select only the words that you think your child might misspell. Pretest your child to find out which words are not yet mastered. Have your child add each word missed on the pretest to his or her Personal Spelling List. When reading your child's writing assignments from school, pay special attention to any words on this list that he or she uses. If you notice any misspellings, make sure to add the words to the Personal Spelling List.

a lot
about
address
all right
already
although
altogether
athlete
aunt
balloon
because
been
beginning
bought
breakfast
breath
built
calendar
captain
caught
cereal
chocolate
choose
coming
committee
cough
could
course
cousin
dear

didn't
disappoint
does
dollar
double
doubt
drawer
early
either
enough
except
favorite
February
field
forty
fourth
friend
fuel
guard
guess
half
haven't
hear
heard
height
here
hour
instead
instinct
maybe

missile
mountain
necessary
neighbor
nickel
no one
o'clock
once
oxygen
patience
people
physical
piece
pleasant
please
poison
possible
potatoes
principal
quarter
receive
rhyme
rhythm
rough
route
said
says
school
separate
similar

sincerely
straight
surprise
swimming
syllable
system
temperature
their
there
they're
thorough
though
thought
threw
through
tomorrow
trouble
Tuesday
until
visible
weather
Wednesday
weigh
we're
where
which
whole
women
would
you're

Appendix C

75 Commonly Confused Words

Students frequently get confused about which word to use even when they know proper spellings. Your child may know how to spell *their*, for example, but still uses the word incorrectly in a sentence: "I want the doughnut over <u>their</u>." Some of these confusing words are *homophones* (words that sound the same but have different spellings and meanings, e.g., *steal* and *steel*), and others are near misses (e.g., *affect* and *effect*). Your child's spelling will improve significantly after he or she learns these commonly confused words.

When choosing words from this list, select only the words that you think your child might misspell. Pretest to find out which words are not mastered.

Have your child add each word missed on this list to his or her Personal Spelling List. When reading your child's writing assignments from school, pay special attention to the words from this list that he or she uses. If you notice any misspellings, make sure to add these words to the Personal Spelling List.

Have your child write any misspelled words in complete sentences, pairing the misspelling with the commonly confused word(s). Tell your child to use the words so that each defines itself in terms of the other. For example: "They're (John and Jan) working on their own project over there by their desk" is better than "They're working on their project over there," because the meaning of each key spelling word is *shown*, not just used.

accept, except
affect, effect
advice, advise
aloud, allowed
already, all ready
assistance,
assistants
began, begin
beginner,
beginning
belief, believe
board, bored
brake, break
breath, breathe
buy, by
cereal, serial
choose, chose
dairy, diary
dear, deer
desert, dessert

dew, do, due
for, four
forty, fourth
groan, grown
hear, here
hole, whole
hoping, hopping
its, it's
knot, not
know, no
lead, led
loose, lose
maybe, may be
meat, meet
medal, metal
moral, morale
naval, navel
passed, past
peace, piece
patience, patients

plain, plane
personal,
personnel
principal, principle
porpoise, purpose
proceed, precede
rain, reign, rein
real, reel
right, write
road, rode, rowed
root, route
sail, sale
scene, seen
scent, sent, cent
sea, see
seam, seem
sense, since
sew, so, sow
shone, shown
sight, site

some, sum
son, sun
steal, steel
straight, strait
symbol, cymbal
there, their, they're
thorough, through
though, thought
threw, through
throne, thrown
tide, tied
to, too, two
trail, trial
weather, whether
wear, were, where
which, witch
who's, whose
your, you're

Outlaw Words

Unfortunately, many of the most often used words are not spelled as they sound. Many are Anglo-Saxon words with pronunciations that have changed often over the years. This group of common words should be memorized as "outlaws," or sight spelling words. The following list includes irregular spelling words that present the greatest problems for intermediate age students.

When choosing words from this list, select only those that you think your child might misspell. Pretest to find out which words are not yet mastered.

Have your child add each word missed on this list to his or her Personal Spelling List. When reading your child's writing assignments from school, pay special attention to the words he or she uses that are on this list. If you notice any misspellings, add those words to the Personal Spelling List.

Help your child memorize these words since sounding out these words will not help.

above	father	money	there
again	floor	month	they
against	four	mother	thought
almost	friend	move	through
already	from	muscle	touch
another	front	nothing	tough
answer	give	ocean	truth
any	gone	often	two
beautiful	great	one	usual
been	guess	only	very
bought	guy	other	walk
break	half	people	want
build	have	pretty	water
busy	heard	prove	were
buy	heart	rough	what
clothes	height	said	where
come	hour	says	who
cough	island	school	whole
could	laugh	should	whose
country	learn	some	wolf
does	listen	son	won
door	live	straight	work
doubt	lose	sure	world
enough	love	talk	would
eye	many	their	your

Common Prefixes and Suffixes

Affixes consist of prefixes and suffixes. *Prefixes* are word parts at the beginnings of words. *Suffixes* are word parts at the ends of words. The following list combines the most useful and frequent Greek and Latin affixes. These prefixes and suffixes add to base or root words to create thousands of words. Prefixes and suffixes are usually unaccented syllables. Help your child practice these spellings both to improve accuracy and to learn to recognize them as syllable parts. Being familiar with the spellings of these affixes will also help your child be able to better identify what is left over—the root, which carries the meaning of the word. Watch out for misspelled prefixes and suffixes in your child's writing. Add any misspelled words using these affixes to your child's personal spelling list.

Prefixes

alti
anti
arch
ac
ab
ad
auto
be
bene
bi
bio
by
chrom
chron
cir
co
con
com
cur
dif
dis
em
en
ex
extra
fac
for
fore
hemi
hyper
il
im
in
inter
intra
intro
ir

ject
micro
mid
mis
nect
non
pan
para
per
peri
phono
photo
phys
psych
por
post
pre
pro
semi
sub
sum
super
sur
syn
tele
trans
tri
ultra
un
under
ves
with

Suffixes

able
ade
age
al
ance

ant
arium
ar
ary
ate
ble
cle
chy
cial
cian
cious
cide
crat
dle
dom
ean
ect
eer
ent
en
eous
ern
ery
ess
est
ette
eth
eus
en
fer
fit
ful
fied
gle
hood
ia
ial
ible

ic
ict
ify
ile
ine
ise
ish
ity
kin
kle
let
ly
ment
ness
nym
ous
or
ory
ose
ple
some
ship
tle
tion
tude
ture
tious
tor
tial
uce
ule
ute
vade
vent
ward
ways
wright
y

Answers

CHAPTER 2

Amazing Anagrams, p. 13
1. chief; 2. ceiling; 3. weight; 4. friend; 5. tried

Crazy Maze, p. 14
START-reign-foreign-neither-niece-cashier-field-ceiling-either-pier-eight-**END**

Wacky Word Sort, p. 15
"i" Before "e:" relief, soldier, chief, field, view, niece, friend; **Except After "c:"** receive, ceiling, conceive, perceive, receipt; **Sounding Like $\bar{a}$:** neighbor, sleigh, weight, eight, beige, freight; **Weirdo Words:** weird, their, either, height, caffeine, neither, forfeit.

Say the Secret Word, pp. 18–19
1. cage; 2. rouge; 3. huge; 4. nudge; 5. stage; 6. Fudge; 7. large; 8. badge; 9. sage; 10. pledge; 11. bridge; 12. dodge; 13. teenager; 14. pages; 15. edge; 16. judge
Secret Word: counterespionage (means secret spying to catch spies!)

Circle and Boxing Match, p. 20

b(a)dge; (a)ge; f(u)dge; r(i)dge; h(u)ge; b[a]rge; pl(e)dge; br(i)dge;

(e)dge; s[ei]ge; r[ou]ge; c[a]ge; l[a]rge; j(u)dge; p[a]ge; s[a]ge

The Secret Code, p. 23
The kitchen counter is a curious place to keep a lighted candle.

Pyramid Power, p. 24
1. I; 2. key; 3. king; 4. cough; 5. camera; 6. curious; 7. calendar; 8. kilometer; 9. confidence; 10. concentrate; 11. kindergarten

Wacky Word Sort, p. 25
"k" column: kitchen, keg, kelp; **"c" column:** catch, cold, cactus, cork, castle, comb

The Fix-It Shop, p. 28
boy, enjoy, employ, joint, poison, choice, joined

Connect the Letters, p. 29
1. corduroy; 2. cowboy; 3. destroy; 4. avoid; 5. foil; 6. spoil; 7. convoy; 8. join; 9. appoint; 10. buoy; 11. overjoy; 12. moist

CHAPTER 3

Brain Teasers, p. 33
1. itch; 2. rich; 3. much; 4. crutch; 5. coach; 6. poach

Hidden Pattern, p. 34
Shaded words: approach, pitcher, match, touch, punch, ranch, fetch, etching, scratched, peach, clutching, hutches

Rhymes and Reasons, pp. 37–38
1. Yes, mess; 2. hiss, miss; 3. boss, loss; 4. grass, gas; 5. cough, off; 6. bus, us; 7. tough, cuff; 8. bull, full; 9. roll, toll; 10. buzz, fuzz

Backward (drawkcaB) Story, p. 39
There once was a very mean <u>bull</u>. He would <u>hiss</u> and snort, then <u>roll</u> in the <u>grass</u>, which he ate until was <u>full</u>. He was definitely <u>boss</u> of his field. One day a <u>yellow</u> bus came and the driver stepped on the gas to chase him <u>off</u>. What a tough <u>loss</u> for his cows! They will really <u>miss</u> their <u>bull</u>.

Lucky Duck, p. 41
This is the story of a little yellow du<u>ck</u> named Lu<u>ck</u>y. He li<u>k</u>ed to soa<u>k</u> his long ne<u>ck</u> in the shallow waters under the histori<u>c</u> do<u>ck</u> on Millers Pond. One day, while swimming under the do<u>ck</u>, Lu<u>ck</u>y heard a franti<u>c</u> scream. Lu<u>ck</u>y loo<u>k</u>ed up qui<u>ck</u>ly to see a boy who had just crashed his bi<u>k</u>e. When the du<u>ck</u> tried to loo<u>k</u> ba<u>ck</u> down, she found that her bill was stu<u>ck</u> between the do<u>ck</u> boards. In a pani<u>c</u>, Lu<u>ck</u>y began to qua<u>ck</u> loudly. A nice tru<u>ck</u> driver heard the noise while driving by and stopped to help. He too<u>k</u> apart the boards to rescue Lu<u>ck</u>y. Lu<u>ck</u>y's bill hurt for a wee<u>k</u>, but she still tells this dramati<u>c</u> story to attentive young du<u>ck</u>lings on Millers Pond.

Wacky Word Sort, p. 42
ck: quickly, stacker, neck, black, wreck, back, quacked; **c (s):** mosaic, terrific, dramatic, historic, frantic, classic, specific; **k (long vowel):** make, baking, raking, taken, bike, hiking, taken; **k (vowel sounds that aren't short):** took, looked, leaked, week, weaken, soak, book

Plurals on the Farm, p. 44
Correct spellings: lives, tomatoes, shelves, duties, wives, videos

Wacky Word Sort, p. 45
1. desks, faces; 2. monkeys, plays; 3. patios, studios; 4. benches, dishes; 5. echoes, tomatoes; 6. berries, cities; 7. lives, wolves

Matching Mania, p. 48
1. until; 2. careful; 3. almost; 4. helpful; 5. always; 6. fulfill

Amazing Anagrams, p. 49
1. spoonful; 2. peaceful; 3. already; 4. powerful; 5. almost; 6. always

Wacky Word Sort, p. 53
Ending begins with vowel: making, nicer, skating, sized; **Ending begins with consanant:** purely, excitement, squarely, hopeless; **"able" or "ous" after soft *c* or *g*:** outrageous, changeable; **Root word ends in "ee," "oe," or "ye:"** agreement, shoestring

To Change or Not to Change, p. 56
1. no, stayed; 2. yes, carries; 3. no, boys; 4. no, trying; 5. yes, cherries; 6. no, enjoyment; 7. no, babyish; 8. no, playful

Wacky Word Sort, p. 57
1. saying (vowel, then "y"); 2. toys (vowel, then "y"); 3. journeyed (vowel, then "y"); 4. carrying (consonant, then "y" but ending starts with "i"); 5. cried (consonant, then "y"); 6. player (vowel, then "y"); 7. flying (consonant, then "y" but ending starts with "i"); 8. driest (consonant, then "y")

CHAPTER 4

To Double or Not to Double, p. 60
3. 1, 2, 3, funny; 4. 1, 2, 3, beginning; 5. 1, 2, 3, forgettable; 6. 2, 3, stacking; 7. 2, 3, lighted; 8. 1,2, comical; 9. 1, 2, 3, permitted

Wacky Word Sort, p. 64
1. arrogance, vacant; 2. radiance, tolerant; 3. clearance, endurance; 4. negligence, coincidence; 5. confidence, providence; 6. reverence, adherence

Circle and Say, p. 66
New words will vary. Examples shown here.
1. b; irritant; circle ance, ant, ancy
2. f; interference; circle ence
3. e; confidence; circle ence, ent, ency

4. d; indulgent; circle ence, ent, ency

5. c; assurance; circle ance, ant, ancy

6. a; expectant; circle ant; Note: the hard *c* or *g* can often be followed by a consonant, but still signals the "a" endings.

Wacky Word Sort, p. 69

1. huggable, applicable; 2. huggable, usable, comparable, applicable, accessible (an exception), laughable, dependable; 3. eligible, reducible; 4. audible, eligible, terrible; 5. usable, comparable, reducible (an exception); 6. applicable; 7. accessible

Circle and Say, p. 71

1. d; visible

2. b; breakable

3. b, e; excusable

4. a, b, f; applicable

5. d; edible

6. b, e, f; adorable

7. c; forcible

8. d; legible

9. a, b; tugable

10. g; confessible

Note to parents: #7 force (forcible) is spelled with "ible" because of the soft *c*, but it is a complete root word and ends in silent "e," which usually indicate "able" endings.

Unscrambled Words, p. 74

confusion, physician, emigration

Hidden Words, p. 76

M	N	I	L	T	U	N	F	C	R	C	A	E
A	U	X	E	F	U	L	E	R	L	R	X	Z
N	A	S	C	R	E	A	T	I	O	N	L	V
S	H	I	I	A	R	N	O	I	T	C	N	U
I	N	A	I	C	I	R	T	C	E	L	E	M
O	W	I	X	T	I	M	B	S	A	X	E	C
N	R	K	I	I	N	A	S	N	M	E	A	P
U	T	O	P	O	Z	I	N	B	L	J	I	W
M	C	E	L	N	O	I	S	S	I	M	I	P

Wacky Word Sort, p. 77

zyun **sound:** confusion, explosion; **"l" or "s" with** *shun* **sound:** illusion, permission, transmission, passion, compulsion, mission; **Person:** musician, physician, magician, beautician, technician; **Most other:** vacation, transition, position, potion, presentation, creation, evolution, information, lotion, education, condition, perforation

CHAPTER 5

Sort and Spell, pp. 94–95
1. presume, preview, prefix, precipitate, prevaricate
2. slowly, highly, partly, seriously
3. blue, clique, clueless
4. miscellaneous, filibuster, carefully
5. checking, struck, sticker
6. tart, bun

CHAPTER 6

The Sound-Spelling Chart Challenge, p. 102
1. three; 2. *u*; 3. one; 4. another letter(s); 5. jump; 6. long *e* and *i*; 7. long *e*; 8. __oo, __ow, __oy

Check It Out, p. 106
1. pain; 2. checkers; 3. leap; 4. elephant; 5. light; 6. ledge; 7. knife; 8. float; 9. write; 10. bird

Three Little Peegz? p. 108
Once upon a time, there were these three little pigs that lived in the same place. Actually, they lived in their own homes in the village. One of these houses was made of straw, another of sticks, with the best one built out of bricks.

One morning, the village wolf came to blow these pigs' houses down. The first ones came down easy, but the brick house wouldn't fall. The dumb wolf climbed up on the roof and jumped down the chimney. The three little pigs had a boiling pot waiting in the fireplace. The wolf fell in the pot and the pigs ate him for lunch.

The End

Mary and the Spooky House, pp. 109–111
Late every night, Mary Piper set out on a long and familiar walk around her neighborhood. She passed the old elementary school, waved at Mrs. Walters, who was turning on her porch light, and then crossed the driveway of the fire station. Nothing seemed out of the ordinary on that deep, dark night in February of 1999.

At the corner of 3rd and Elm, Mary thought she heard a soft, wailing cry down the street. Turning off her usual path, she began walking down Elm Street to investigate. This was a decision that she would later regret.

Elm Street was in an older section of town. Its tall trees swayed in the moonlight and cast taller shadows against the two-story homes lining the street. Not a soul was to be seen or heard. Mary slowed her walk and tried to convince herself that the soft, wailing cry was only the sound of the wind through the trees. She began to turn around for home, when a louder cry pierced the night. Mary stopped, dead in her tracks.

The sound seemed to come from the top story of the house at the end of the street. Mary wheeled around, and then broke into a run. Mary did not slow to a walk until her feet touched her front lawn. She slept poorly that night, tossing and turning until dawn.

That morning, Mary read in the newspaper that the very house at the end of Elm Street that so frightened her the night before was being torn down in order to connect Elm Street to the center of town. Perhaps the wailing sound that Mary heard was the house's last wailing cry about leaving Elm Street forever.

My E-Male, p. 113

I know someone named Spell Check.
He lives in my PC.
He's always there to try and help
When I hit a wrong key.
But when I write an e-mail,
On him I can't depend.
I need to also proofread
Before I push the SEND.

The E-Mail I Wish I Hadn't Sent, p. 114

Dear Martha,

I'm so sad about what has happened to you! I've never seen such a huge waste, but their loss will be your gain. At least now I'll get to see more of you. Remember, good things come to those who wait.

Your Friend, Through Thick and Thin,

John

P.S. Cheer up. You'll find another job soon.

Index